ENGAGING STUDENT VOICES IN THE
STUDY OF TEACHING AND LEARNING

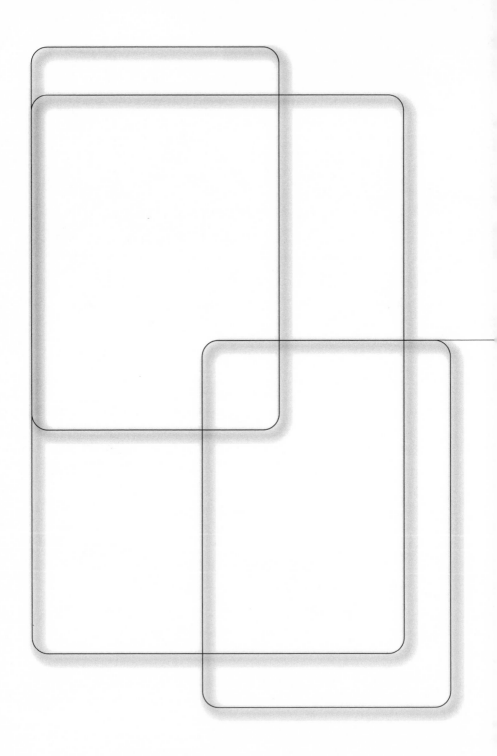

ENGAGING STUDENT VOICES IN THE STUDY OF TEACHING AND LEARNING

Edited by

Carmen Werder and

Megan M. Otis

Foreword by Pat Hutchings and Mary Taylor Huber

STERLING, VIRGINIA

COPYRIGHT © 2010 BY STYLUS PUBLISHING, LLC.

Published by Stylus Publishing, LLC
22883 Quicksilver Drive
Sterling, Virginia 20166-2102

Library of Congress Cataloging-in-Publication-Data
Engaging student voices in the study of teaching and learning / edited by Carmen Werder and Megan M. Otis ; foreword by Pat Hutchings and Mary Taylor Huber.
—1st ed.
   p. cm.
  Includes bibliographical references and index.
  ISBN 978-1-57922-419-6 (cloth : alk. paper)
  ISBN 978-1-57922-420-2 (pbk. : alk. paper)
  1. College teaching—United States.   2. Learning.
  I. Werder, Carmen, 1946–   II. Otis, Megan M. (Megan Michelle), 1983–
LB2331.E655   2010
378.1'25—dc22   2009025827

13-digit ISBN: 978-1-57922-419-6 (cloth)
13-digit ISBN: 978-1-57922-420-2 (paper)

Printed in the United States of America

All first editions printed on acid free paper
that meets the American National Standards Institute
Z39-48 Standard.

Bulk Purchases

Quantity discounts are available for use in workshops and for staff development.
Call 1-800-232-0223

First Edition, 2010

10 9 8 7 6 5 4 3 2 1

To all those teachers and learners who have had the courage to hear each others' voices and to all those who have not yet been heard. And especially to our favorite little learners—Cameron, Pace, and Elsie—know now that your voices matter.

CONTENTS

ACKNOWLEDGMENTS

We thank the many people who have contributed their voices to the thinking behind this book even if they're not official co-authors. First off, we wouldn't have even begun this whole conversation had it not been for the Carnegie Academy for the Scholarship of Teaching and Learning (CASTL), so we offer special thanks to our CASTL gurus Lee Shulman, Pat Hutchings, Mary Taylor Huber, Richard Gale, and Tony Ciccone.

We also have other CASTL companions who have travelled this journey with us but do not show up in the table of contents, including the participants in the 2003–2006 Student Voices cluster and in the 2006–2009 Institutional Leadership Student Voices group.

From Western Washington University: Dayo Anderson, Kelly Barefield, Andrew Bodman, Kris Bulcroft, Rachel Christman, Leslie Driediger, Whitney Dunbar, Craig Dunn, Mercedes Elg, Joe Garcia, Glenn Gilliam, Peter Moe, Karen Morse, Leslie Napora, and Kari Painter.

From California State University, Long Beach: Terre Allen, Joseph Baclig, Heather Carter, Margaret Costa, Michael Glassoff, William Harkness, Elizabeth Hoffman, Corey Johnson, William Johnson, Asma Mana, James Mateik, Tina Matuchniak, Troy Mitchell, Kaori Mizukami, Cerah O'Grady, Deanna Palmer, Bryce Peterson, Julie Rivera, Mami Saito, Parvin Shariat, Nancy Sheley, Jennifer Smith, Mary Taverner, Marcy Walter, Kira Wilson, Sunny Yoshimura, and William Younglove.

From North Seattle Community College: Koby Allan, Jack Bautsch, Sam Bellomio, Suki Bourquin, Haley Gronbeck, Jim Harnish, Jane Lister Reiss, Jim Patterson, Cate Overstreet, and Heidi Wilken.

From the University of Maryland, College Park: Spencer Benson, Chip DeAtley, Jo Paoletti, Eden Segal, Chuck Sternheim, Jessica Toole, and Rochelle Tractenberg.

From University of Washington, Bothell: Becky Reed Rosenberg, Jerelyn Resnick, and Kimberly Shay.

And from University of Nevada, Las Vegas: our dear, departed friend Leora Baron.

FOREWORD

We are honored to provide a foreword to this volume and to be part of the story behind it. A decade ago, the Carnegie Foundation for the Advancement of Teaching began a program aimed at strengthening teaching and learning in college and university classrooms. The Carnegie Academy for the Scholarship of Teaching and Learning (CASTL) invited educators from the full range of disciplines and fields and from all institutional types to turn their scholarly habits and skills to their work as teachers. From the beginning one of the defining features of their efforts, elaborated on in our work as two of the program's organizers, was a clear focus on student learning. As we wrote in *The Advancement of Learning* (Huber & Hutchings, 2005), powerful things happen when faculty treat their classrooms as a site for inquiry, exploring "questions in their own teaching—and especially in their students' learning" in ways that colleagues can build on (p. ix).

But the notion that students might be active participants in such work was not immediately obvious, and Carnegie called on scholars to find more and better ways of engaging students in discussions and inquiry about learning. We were not alone. Across the country people were beginning to explore possibilities for such involvement. Reporting on a situation that must have occurred elsewhere as well, colleagues at Western Washington University trace the origins of their collaborative programs to a CASTL event where an observant faculty participant (William Lay, co-author of chapter 5) asked, "Where are the students?" What it means to take that question seriously is the subject of this volume.

The first of the book's two parts, "Foundations," includes five chapters that explore the theoretical and conceptual dimensions of student voices in the scholarship of teaching and learning. Issues of power and authority in the classroom figure prominently here, and "essential questions about meaning making and identity are inextricably linked to how students do their work and think about their education" (see chapter 1, p. 8). As this quotation from

Stephen Bloch-Schulman suggests, the ideas and examples in *Engaging Student Voices* are powerfully propelled by values: a commitment to more shared responsibility for learning among students and teachers, a more democratic intellectual community, and more authentic *co-inquiry*. The authors not only describe these commitments, they enact them. *Engaging Student Voices* is co-edited by a faculty-student pair, and 8 of its 11 chapters, as well as the conclusion, are co-authored by faculty and students—a collaborative spirit evident in the structure of their arguments as well. Consider, for instance, the twin testimonies of a student and a faculty member from Elon University in chapter 1, and the "parlor talk" among faculty and students from Western Washington University in chapter 2. This volume truly "walks the walk."

At the same time, the foundations of this work have a pragmatic side—a concern with making the scholarship of teaching and learning more *useful*. Indeed, as pointed out in chapter 3 by anthropologists Megan Otis and Joyce Hammond, the impulse to involve students in the scholarship of teaching and learning can be seen as part of a larger move to open the process of knowledge building to a wider group of participants, and to expand our conception of who has expertise to contribute. As a form of participatory action research, Otis and Hammond argue, the scholarship of teaching and learning is a move to connect theory and practice more firmly to ensure that all voices are heard and valued and to draw on "students' *insider* knowledge of their expertise as learners" (p. 32). Doing so, as this volume makes clear, is not only a right idea, it is a practical one because as Elon University student Kelly Flannery puts it in chapter 1, "*how* one gathers information matters because the methods of gathering information determine the viability and value of the information gathered" (p. 12).

The second half of the volume, "Enactment," goes on to explore what these methods look like and what fruit they bear, beginning with a useful overview by colleagues from Illinois State University about "the continuum of student roles . . . from simply serving as research subjects in a SoTL [scholarship of teaching and learning] study to working as an independent SoTL researcher" (see chapter 6, p. 84). At Elon, for instance, involving students in the scholarship of teaching and learning has taken the form of student-faculty partnerships around curricular design and redesign (see chapters 7 and 8). Case studies from Teachers of English to Speakers of Other Languages, teacher education, composition, and statistics point to the value of inviting, and in some cases requiring, students to mine their own experiences as learners for insights and advice about course design, readings, requirements, and assessment. This work brings the principles and benefits of the broader undergraduate research movement to the topic of teaching and learning.

A different approach has emerged at Eastern Michigan University. Political science professor Jeffrey Bernstein tells the story of inviting students to serve as facilitators of a complex simulation in his American government course, and how that role gradually expands to full-fledged co-inquiry into the course and its impact on disciplinary learning and other outcomes such as leadership development. As Bernstein and his student co-authors point out, the greatest gains have come from the experience of student ownership, when the course and the inquiry into it become their project rather than his alone. This experience is not, of course, unique. The Illinois State University authors of chapter 10 report that student researchers' sense of themselves as independent learners increased as a result of taking more responsible roles in their scholarship of teaching and learning project teams.

These stories and others in the volume offer a variety of lessons. For starters, readers will find suggestions about more nitty-gritty matters of student voices and involvement: the value of food (for example, pretzels have been an important element at Western Washington University) or of finding a neutral space to share ideas (Elon faculty and students met together over morning coffee and at lunch). At a more conceptual level, there are important lessons about the range and variety of ways that students have been engaged in this work, be it in what Carmen Werder terms *conversational scholarship* (see chapter 2) or in the development of more formal written studies. We can imagine a college where opportunities for such work would be threaded throughout the curriculum. Not every student would be fully engaged in the scholarship of teaching and learning in every course, certainly, but he or she would encounter different kinds of involvement at different points in the curriculum in ways that add up to a qualitatively different and more powerful educational experience. Making such opportunities available is important because as this volume also makes clear, this is transformational work—work that changes people.

We think of Christopher Manor, a student co-author featured in chapter 1, whose involvement in more collaborative forms of work on teaching and learning moves him from an almost breathtaking level of disengagement ("the thought of actively trying to learn something never crossed my mind";

see p. 5) to a deep sense of responsibility not only for his own education but for contributing to the learning of his classmates. Faculty, too, recount transformative experiences. Colleagues at North Seattle Community College say, "[our engagement with students] transformed our pedagogy and transformed our conceptions of what we do as leaders and participants in education" (see chapter 11, p. 162). Others write of paradigm shifts, turning points, new insights, and changes in classroom culture.

These are powerful claims. Colleges and universities are often seen as hidebound, and glacierlike in their resistance to change; metaphors of turning a battleship or moving a graveyard have become well-worn clichés. But what we see in *Engaging Student Voices* is the possibility of a very positive kind of climate change in which, in Jeffrey Bernstein's phrase, "teachers do less, students more." Such a shift is not easy, as he and the co-authors of chapter 4 remind us: Teachers and students alike testify to frustrations, to difficult negotiations of new roles and expectations, to deep dilemmas about appropriate boundaries, and to ethical issues raised by student involvement in the scholarship of teaching and learning.

In spite of these challenges, and as the volume's diverse group of authors make clear, an expanded conception of the student role in the scholarship of teaching and learning clearly brings significant benefits for those involved. But there's another benefit as well. What most heartens us as observers of the larger movement is how the involvement of students brings the scholarship of teaching and learning full circle, back to what we would argue is its real home and purpose: strengthening what goes on every day between faculty and students in classrooms and other settings.

This purpose, "invoking the *L*" (as Jane Verner and William Lay call it in chapter 5), is manifest throughout the volume, and it is embodied with particular eloquence in chapter 11 by Tom Drummond and Kalyn Shea Owens who tell the story of "capturing student learning" around a key concept (charge distribution) in a chemistry course. This is challenging work: students are videotaped in small-group sessions, and the video is turned into a PowerPoint "capture" of still photographs and transcript excerpts. These in turn are shared with the full class and employed as grist for discussion. Drummond and Owens offer a number of reflections on the process. "It is shocking," they say in, "how little faculty know about what actually happens for students during the act of learning" (p. 176). But also clear is the power for students and faculty alike of looking closely at the twists and turns, the messy, emergent business of moving from not knowing to fuller understanding—and doing so in a community in which learners, according to Drummond and Owens, "see themselves as people who figured things out together":

> We all face the need for something to examine together, something specific, complex, and nuanced to reflect upon, to honor the differences in the way each of us perceives the world and expresses ideas. We all face the problems of working cooperatively together, of solving problems, of examining habitual practices, bringing self-critical awareness of our own uncertainties, and of offering, in mutual comfort, tentative conjectures and hypotheses. We all face co-creating a future through our interactions in the present. We all face an expectation that we wish to move toward an ideal, a beautiful dream of our own abilities to do well. (p. 183)

It is hard to imagine a better statement of the promise of the scholarship of teaching and learning. Readers will bring their own experiences, questions, even skepticism to this collection, but we hope they will take from it, as we do, an expanded and more nuanced sense of the roles that students can play in this work and a renewed sense of hope and the possibility that this work can enrich the educational experience of students—and teachers—as well.

Pat Hutchings and Mary Taylor Huber
Carnegie Foundation for the Advancement of Teaching

Reference

Huber, M. T., & Hutchings, P. (2005). *The advancement of learning: Building the teaching commons*. San Francisco: Jossey-Bass.

PART ONE

FOUNDATIONS

FOUNDATIONS OF STUDENT-FACULTY PARTNERSHIPS IN THE SCHOLARSHIP OF TEACHING AND LEARNING

Theoretical and Developmental Considerations

*Christopher Manor, Stephen Bloch-Schulman,
Kelly Flannery, and Peter Felten*

The process of writing a chapter about student-faculty partnerships (like the practice of such partnerships in the scholarship of teaching and learning [SoTL]) is no simple task. Who sets the agenda? Which "voice" should be heard most clearly in the text? Faculty have experience writing such chapters and can draw on disciplinary and pedagogical expertise. Those assets, however, obscure what students bring (and faculty lack) in writing about student-faculty partnerships. Students know from direct and ongoing personal experience how power and partnership are expressed and practiced in the classroom in a way that often remains invisible to faculty, even as faculty set the ground rules for this relationship. As standpoint theorists and phenomenologists often remind us, deep understanding of a situation only develops when *all* relevant perspectives are honored, not just those with power and authority; and they remind us that this inclusiveness is particularly important when those most affected by power dynamics are those least likely to have a voice to express and change those dynamics (Harding, 2004).

In an effort to honor multiple perspectives, we begin with parallel commentaries, one by Christopher Manor and one by Stephen Bloch-Schulman. Chris is a sophomore at Elon University who has worked with Stephen in a class and as an undergraduate researcher. Stephen is an assistant professor of philosophy at Elon. Following these commentaries, Kelly Flannery develops the chapter's theoretical argument. She is a senior at Elon and has been in class (as student and as co-teacher) and has been working on SoTL projects with Stephen for the past 2 years. Peter Felten, who directs Elon's Center for the Advancement of Teaching and Learning, concludes the chapter with a reflection on student-faculty partnerships in the context of existing SoTL literature.

On Development: Moving Into Co-Authorship

We (Chris and Stephen) have decided to present our commentaries in parallel, side-by-side form with related subtitles. We chose this format intentionally to show as best we could that neither voice has priority. Both are necessary, and to put one before the other cannot but imply a greater importance. At the same time, we appreciate the traditional convention of reading from left to right, so we have—to make sure the student voice is heard fully—deliberately placed the student commentary in the left column. In our commentaries we try to show how our experiences have transformed us. Each of us begins with a traditional view of teaching and learning and our roles therein then move through a middle view into a more fully realized view. Chris begins by reflecting on his own assumptions about education, then becomes open to student/teacher collaboration, and only later moves to student-student collaboration; Stephen shifts from a traditional faculty standpoint to one that focuses on student-student collaboration, and only later considers more innovative student-teacher collaboration. This difference speaks to our points of view and experiences, our habits and our expectations of academic work. Our commentaries reveal how we have moved toward work we find more authentic and more meaningful, and in each case, this movement has meant becoming more collaborative.

An Examination of the Theoretical Foundations of Student Voices in SoTL From a Student's Perspective

KELLY FLANNERY

Bringing student voices into the process of teaching and learning has an undeniably transformative effect. Chris traces this influence in showing how he no

On Student Development: Moving Into Co-Authorship

CHRISTOPHER MANOR

In my essay, I draw primarily from my personal experience, focusing on what I came to believe my education is truly about and what happened when I began to take ownership of it.

To this day Stephen (the guy on the other side of the page) is the only teacher who has asked me what I wanted to get out of taking a class. Ever. I had never even thought about it: what I want to get out of a class, how does this class relate to me? I grew up thinking what I assumed every other student thought and the majority of students still think—what do I want to get out of this class? An A. The thought of actively trying to learn something never crossed my mind.

Then one day as we were discussing this chapter, we happened upon the subject of teacher and student responsibility and then *wham!* the realization hit me: What were my own responsibilities for my education? It was such an odd question. Why had I not thought of this before?

The more I thought about it, the more it shook up everything I associated with education and learning; how I had done homework, written papers—everything has been completely turned on end. I had been watching my education pass me by without ever taking part. I struggled with this question (and still do) because I had never been confronted with taking responsibility for my own education.

My conception of the work I was doing as a student had been completely inside out. Realizing this, I decided to change it. Instead of thinking about papers as required work, I began thinking about what I wanted to authentically learn

On Faculty Development: Moving Into Co-Authorship

STEPHEN BLOCH-SCHULMAN

In his essay, "The Amateur in the Operating Room: History and the Scholarship of Teaching and Learning," David Pace (2004) points out there are "two forms of knowledge" at work in any classroom activity, "knowledge of the subject matter, and knowledge of how it may be taught and learned" (p. 1171). He makes this point to show us—as disciplinary experts and teachers—how our own disciplinary expertise is often not transferred into our teaching: Where we would consult with other experts in our own field, we tend to teach in isolation; where we look at the most current research as we do our own disciplinary work, we rely on folk beliefs about the classroom and base our teaching practices on "knowledge that would have been unremarkable fifty years ago" (p. 1171). He dares us to see the incongruity of our deep care, respect, and critical engagement in our disciplinary research in contrast—all too often—to our lack of these in our teaching.

My goal here is to highlight Pace's (2004) argument, in particular, in the context of SoTL. Furthermore, I seek to show how my own research in SoTL has changed through my involvement with students as co-researchers and through some of the larger insights they can offer. I explore these themes by describing my own developmental stages, starting as the novice teacher Pace describes as the amateur to one who does SoTL in a scholarly way and finally to one who takes it as his task to more fully integrate the theoretical and methodological commitments he has gained in his discipline to his teaching and his SoTL research.

from the assignment. I could now see why we have papers. They finally made sense.

Student-Teacher Collaboration

This new concept was liberating, revolutionary. I went to my English professor to discuss what I had discovered about taking responsibility for my education. I wanted to see if his goals for the course were the same as mine. To my surprise, now that I actually had goals for the course, they were exactly the same as *his*! Then I asked what he expected and wanted us to learn from an upcoming paper. I could not have been more pleased with the results.

Because I had met with him and discussed the issue, I completely understood the assignment, why he assigned it, and exactly what I would learn from it. I no longer viewed the assignment as something I would do for him; it was something I would do for me, as practice with a new critical approach to literature. The reason for grading it was so he could help me see if I was on the right track.

I went to my other professors as well and was met with similar helpful and co-operative attitudes. Each teacher I explained this idea to was more than willing to help me with concepts I did not quite understand and to clarify what their goals were for each assignment. They had been willing to work with me all along; I just had to meet them halfway. I finally understood why partnerships in teaching and learning are so crucial. To be able to learn from my professors I had to be mature enough to want something besides grades and a diploma from my education. But something still puzzled me. Why had I shirked these responsibilities

When I came to teaching, I came with a certain set of theoretical and methodological commitments that had been honed through years of course work, examinations, and dialogue. At the time, I was writing about Hannah Arendt's conceptions of personal and political responsibility and phenomenology, deconstruction, democratic theory, feminism, and postmodern theory. When I entered the classroom, I wanted to teach these particular theoretical and methodological frameworks to students. But I did so without thinking through how these subjects ought to inform my teaching. For example, though my disciplinary research is in collective responsibility and focuses on the harm of seeing responsibility and freedom as individualist and atomistic, I expected my students to do their work alone, without even consulting others. In addition, I set up the tasks, the criteria, and the timeline; students were expected to follow what I had planned with no say about how the semester and the course ran.

Student-Student Collaboration

As I began to learn what my students could not do independently and came to understand the challenges students were having with the tasks I was asking them to perform, I came to see the possibility of collaborative work in the classroom. This change was in part because of the influence of my dean, James Ruebel of Ball State University, and in part because of a Lumina Foundation for Education re-grant I received to do work in SoTL under Paul Ranieri (also of Ball State University). Through Ruebel's and Ranieri's influences, I began to read voraciously on SoTL and began to experiment with highly collaborative work in classes. I before? Why had they not even occurred to me?

Every day I discover ways my education, and education in general, lack partnership. It is easy for us students to blame our problems on our professors, to say the reason we do not learn is because of them. If I can change my entire concept of education just by thinking of partnerships, I wonder how that single change would affect other students' learning?

Student-Student Collaboration

While student-teacher partnerships are key, student-student collaborations are even more important considering that throughout school we interact far more with each other than with our professors. What I realize now after so many years is that I never really thought about anyone else's education. If I had a thought or opinion about the subject being taught, I kept it to myself. I mean, *I* was learning and that's all that really mattered, right? Wrong. I never imagined that by holding back, I was denying my classmates an important learning opportunity.

Every topic we learn is like a puzzle. Each thought or comment one student has could be the crucial piece another student needs to complete that puzzle. So every question we don't ask hurts not only ourselves but our entire class.

Can you imagine a classroom where students take responsibility for *each other* in addition to just themselves? Can you imagine how much more we would learn, how much we would benefit?

Conclusion

Here's an analogy from medicine that my dad shared to illustrate a similar kind of transformative change. Like professors,

went so far as to have two sections of students in a course work together on a project each student was responsible for, and the project counted for 70% of each student's final grade for the course. This collaborative learning project became the central piece of my SoTL. I was so committed to having students work collaboratively that when I interviewed at Elon University, I spoke about my desire to explore more and more varied ways to have students collaborate—and by that, I now know, I meant: to collaborate with each other on tasks and assignments that I had independently crafted for them to accomplish. This was always collaboration between the students. Furthermore, because I was the one determining how I thought students could learn better— without their input or understanding—I was focused, in the language that Pat Hutchings (2000) uses, on the "what works" questions.

Student-Teacher Collaboration

When I arrived at Elon, I went through another transformation, this time from thinking of collaboration as something students do with other students to something I do with students in learning about teaching and learning. This fundamentally different context prompted this realization. This, I now see, was based on my misunderstanding of, in Hutchings' (2000) language, "what is"— what the students could do, what they were challenged by, how they did their work, and why. The students at Elon are quite different from those I had worked with elsewhere, and these differences made many of the habits I had honed elsewhere counterproductive for teaching very different types of students in this new context. With the help of my colleagues Peter Felten and with the example doctors once were treated like gods. Nurses had to stand when doctors entered the room. Their word was law. Patients left their health up to their doctors because they assumed they didn't have the know-how to take proper care of themselves. But as time went on, people started to ask their doctors more and more questions about their health and to suggest possible causes of their ailments. The doctors were taken aback; what could patients possibly know about medicine? Who were they to ask what should be done about their own bodies?

Enter the age of modern medicine when many people began to rely less on their doctors and more on themselves. I don't want to downplay doctors or make it seem like we don't need them, but healthy living is a partnership: A doctor cannot get you to live a better lifestyle just as you cannot prescribe yourself medicine. Learning is a similar kind of partnership.

I understand that not every teacher or professor will react positively to this way of thinking. Even my dad, in reading this piece, thought I should refer to Stephen as Dr. Schulman since it would seem disrespectful for a student to call a professor by his first name (even though Stephen has asked me to do so). On the other hand, lots of teachers are eager to adopt this partnership model. Of course, teachers have the luxury of time.

I'm already 20 years old and in a couple of years the majority of students who helped write this book will have moved beyond college to be teachers or other professionals. We will no longer know what it's really like to be a student or how students really learn. The study of education will always need newer, more diverse student voices. We need all the help we can get.

set by Deborah Long and Richard Mihans (Mihans, Long, & Felten, 2008) of student/faculty collaborative course redesign, I decided that to get to know *these* students better I would change my SoTL from something *I did* to something that *we do*.

This latest developmental shift has profoundly changed my SoTL work and my teaching. In terms of my research, I have begun to co-author articles with students, including "Student/Faculty Partnerships in Course Re-Design: Learning About Who Students Are to Transform Them," (Schulman, Bright, Duggins, Flannery, & McGarry, 2008). Through collaboration on SoTL projects with students, my research has deepened in important ways. By collaborating with students, I have learned how little I know about what they can do, what challenges them, how they act, what their habits and values are, and how they experience the tasks put to them.

Conclusion

What works? remains the question I most want to have an answer to, but I recognize more and more that it rests on *what is?* and that faculty (myself included) generally know little about what is. As Chris shows in his comments on the left, essential questions about meaning making and identity are inextricably linked to how students do their work and think about their education. These cannot be fairly explored or understood without their voices. Learning *what is* simply is not possible without understanding it from a student's perspective, and thus I see my work in SoTL requiring, more than ever, input from and collaboration with students. In seeing my work this way, I have returned to my disciplinary roots to find that the work I do with critical theory, democratic theory, and feminism now inform and are informed by

The students who wrote this book aren't extraordinary people—our primary asset is that we know firsthand what it's like to be a student. You don't need to have the best grades or take the hardest classes, just be interested in your own education.

It doesn't take a lot to start this kind of conversation with a teacher, just ask one about his or her teaching goals, or why he or she wanted to teach. Just talk to your teachers.

When my English professor and I discussed this chapter he said students have told him they like to learn, but they don't like school. He couldn't quite wrap his mind around the concept, but nearly every student reading this knows what that feels like. Somehow school and learning got separated, and it's up to all of us, professors and students, to reunite them.

the work I do in my SoTL. I have not merely transferred my habits and comportment in my disciplinary research to my teaching, I have successfully eliminated any distinction between the two domains and the research I do in both.

Furthermore, the insights and new habits I have gained by inquiring with students have changed my teaching: Thanks to the work of Caitlin McGarry I focus more on student self-assessment, seeing it as a crucial transferable skill that undergirds self-directed and internally motivated learning (Schulman et al., 2008). I have become more thoughtful about how the feedback I give is interpreted and made meaningful (or not) by students, thanks to the work of Kimberly Duggins (Schulman et al.) I have thought about classroom collaboration in more democratic and self-directed ways, thanks to Kelly Flannery's (Schulman et al.) focus in her SoTL project. And I have asked, along with Durice White, how students can come to be successful in classes in which they dislike or are offended by a teacher. Many of these are questions I was open to, but few are questions I was focused on. In addition, some are questions I would not have asked were it not for students' voices and students' collaboration with me.

longer approaches education with the mentality typical of many students, but has embraced the responsibility he has for his own education and has created academic goals that revolve around learning authentically. Stephen describes how student voices have transformed his teaching and his research in SoTL. I extend these themes by critically examining the traditional classroom and research dynamic to show ways that integrating student voices into SoTL can democratize education by giving voice to students and offering an opportunity for their experiences to more fully inform what happens in the classroom and what happens in research that is focused on what happens in the classroom.

From the point of view of students, the experience of education in the classroom almost always includes a hierarchy with an uneven distribution of power between professors and students. Professors are seen as having a majority of the power to educate, while students most likely see themselves as having secondary or no power. There are good reasons for students to perceive the power as unevenly distributed in favor of the teacher, which is reflected even in something as seemingly innocuous as how the classroom is physically set up.

The teacher's power to educate is not a negative. Professors obviously have much greater expertise in their specific subject than the students and should be viewed as authority figures in that discipline. Their power is an important and necessary aspect for a functioning classroom and for student learning. In addition, they frequently have experience teaching, often knowing what challenges students and what the expectations are for quality work. On the other hand, most students are habituated to believe they are all but totally dependent on the professor. In my experience, many students perceive themselves as practically powerless in their classes. This view is deeply problematic.

The concepts of power and responsibility are intimately connected. Greater power means a greater ability to act and thus a greater sense of responsibility to do so. Similarly, less power (or worse, powerlessness) equates to less ability to act and less responsibility. This correlation between power and responsibility makes the power disparity in the classroom harmful because students believe that teachers hold the power in the classroom; they act as if teachers do, and they see teachers as bearing all or a majority of the responsibility to educate and to produce learning. Or, to put it another way, the students' perceived powerlessness in their own education translates into a lack of their taking responsibility for their own education.

Chris's section illustrates this gap and also reveals two additional common problems that occur when students perceive professors as having the majority of the power and responsibility to educate. First, the assumption that professors possess all the course-related knowledge and that students have none contributes to a fundamental misunderstanding of what it means to learn—that learning essentially is the transfer of knowledge, a finite set of facts, from professor to student, rather than a process that allows examination and making meaning from knowledge. This mistaken assumption reinforces students' sense of powerlessness. All too often, students don't even see their education as *their* education at all; they see it as something done to them rather than something they do. Second, students do not see their fellow classmates as offering unique and valuable perspectives. They rarely see classmates as partners or resources; instead, they are individuals who happen to be receiving knowledge from the same professor. The value of group discussion and collaborative learning is lost when the power/responsibility to educate is seen as resting solely in the hands of the teacher. Years of conditioning have taught students to accept the information bestowed on them by the professor and to dismiss as irrelevant the perspectives of their peers.

This conditioning is why student voices in education and in SoTL are particularly transformative. Inviting students into a learning partnership exemplifies and enacts a radically new idea for most students: Students can offer something to the process of education—a different perspective. Students have unique insight into what it is like to actually be *this* particular student trying to learn and make meaning of *this* particular subject at *this* particular time in *this* particular context. While the professor is rightly considered an expert on the course subject, the student also has a type of expertise that warrants recognition. Using student voices allows students to actively participate in their education and recognize that other people, in conjunction with the professor, can offer a valuable contribution to the classroom. It enables students to perceive themselves and their classmates as having more power in their education and therefore as also having a greater amount of responsibility for it. At the same time, it invites professors to rethink their assumptions about education and students, and to reenvision the classroom as a truly collaborative learning space.

Ultimately then perhaps the most important thing that student voices offer is a way to decentralize the classroom and the SoTL research process. Instead of authority, expertise, power, and responsibility being highly concentrated in the teacher, they are disaggregated among all participants more equally. The recognition of the distributed nature of educational power allows for a more democratic classroom experience and a richer inquiry into teaching and learning.

Although advocates for liberal education frequently cite the goal of developing skills necessary for students to function as democratic citizens (such as critical thinking, recognition and understanding of multiple perspectives, and the employment of scrutiny and reason), the actual teaching that students experience often is resoundingly, even hypocritically, antidemocratic. The ability to understand and imagine many different points of view is an important capacity for students to function well as citizens, but no matter how well tailored the course content is toward cultivating a multiperspective frame of mind, if one perspective—the teacher's—dominates the classroom, then his or her actions blatantly contradict the skills he or she is trying to instill in the students. Conversely, students and teachers acting as partners in education and in research can demonstrate essential skills for citizenship, including the respect of others and others' views.

The gap where the teacher's intention for the lesson fails to meet the student's perception of the lesson is most likely the result of a failure in the student-faculty relationship. There is a lack of dialogue, a lack of reciprocity between the two parties. Thus, a more open conversation between student and professor about the process of teaching and learning and of the meaning of what has been learned would be able to prevent students from learning such underlying, negative messages taught by professors and enable teachers to gain a better understanding of how and what students actually learn from the point of view of the student.

Finally, extending this idea to SoTL research, more fully incorporating student voices could help faculty to be cognizant of and careful about the methods they use as researchers. Just as they may be proclaiming one goal and instilling a different outcome altogether in their classrooms, their research—especially their research into teaching and learning in which they are supposedly fostering civic and humanistic values—needs to be built upon the same principles. Faculty might ask themselves, particularly as they research teaching and learning, not only what questions they should be asking about teaching and learning and how to gather data in this regard, but *who* should be asking the questions and who should be gathering and interpreting the data. That is, as standpoint theorists and phenomenologists show, *how* one gathers information matters because the methods of gathering information determine the viability and value of the information gathered (Harding, 2004). This link is especially true in matters of teaching and learning where the consequences for learning are so important.

An Examination of the Theoretical Foundations of Student Voices in SoTL From a Teaching Center Director

Peter Felten

One reason for faculty to form partnerships with students is to broaden the types of SoTL questions being asked. As Barr and Tagg (1995) wrote more than a decade ago, for too long higher education has focused on teaching and instruction rather than on student learning. Although the shift to a *learning paradigm* has taken hold in many areas of today's higher education, the *instructional paradigm* still holds considerable sway, even among SoTL practitioners. Three of the foundational texts in the SoTL literature illustrate this point. Randy Bass's (1999) excellent article, "The Scholarship of Teaching: What's the Problem?" remains powerful for how it equates research problems with teaching problems: "Changing the status of the *problem* in teaching from terminal remediation to ongoing investigation is precisely what the movement for a scholarship of teaching is all about." Despite the importance of this insight, Bass frames a SoTL problem as the teacher's problem, literally as something a faculty member *has*. Because this problem is the teacher's, it typically begins as a problem of teaching practice rather than a problem of student learning (or a problem that exists in the space between what the teacher and the students do).

Pat Hutchings (2000) builds on Bass's (1999) insights to construct a "taxonomy of questions" in SoTL. The first of these, "where many faculty begin," according to Hutchings, is "what works" (2000, p. 4) questions, focusing on the relative effectiveness of different teaching strategies. Stephen's commentary earlier in the chapter articulates precisely this approach. The attention here is on faculty practice (the instructional paradigm) rather than on student learning or on the space between. Of the other three sorts of questions in Hutchings' taxonomy (what is, visions of the possible, and new frameworks for practice), only one—what is—focuses squarely on student learning. The others attend primarily, or at least initially, to the teacher.

That same year Lee Shulman (2000) posed the question, "Why a scholarship of teaching and learning?" Shulman argued that the practice of SoTL is a professional obligation for all scholars who take seriously their duties as educators. Scholars not only create new knowledge but also share what they have learned; these scholarly habits ought to be practiced not only in the laboratory and library but also in the classroom. Shulman also contended that SoTL helps faculty, as individuals and as a community, to teach in ways that are more effective, reflective, and innovative. Finally, he suggested that SoTL would offer valuable evidence that could be used to guide policy making in higher education.

This faculty-centered focus continues to dominate the SoTL literature. For example, one SoTL guidebook, *Inquiry Into the College Classroom* (Savory, Burnett, & Goodburn, 2007), begins with a telling question: "What is happening in my classroom?" (p. 1). Similarly, Maryellen Weimer's *Enhancing Scholarly Work on Teaching and Learning* (2006) argues persuasively for the need for higher-quality scholarship on teaching and learning and for the centrality of pedagogical scholarship in higher education; still, while presenting many ways to enhance scholarly work on teaching, she essentially ignores the potential of faculty's partnering with students to better understand learning and teaching.

My point is not to condemn SoTL work or its practitioners but to highlight a natural product of faculty-based SoTL: The kinds of questions we ask are often questions about ourselves. Hence, even in the best SoTL research, our answers will often be about ourselves. While we are fascinating folks, and our practice is worthy of careful research, SoTL is not likely to reach its full potential until it opens up the questions at the heart of SoTL inquiry. We can do that by building on the work of our peers, by conducting high-quality research, and through sophisticated theoretical approaches, but we also can do that (perhaps more effectively, perhaps more simply) by creating partnerships with students through the entire SoTL process—not only in the gathering and analysis of evidence but also in asking questions.

References

Barr, R. B., & Tagg, J. (1995). From teaching to learning: A new paradigm for undergraduate education. *Change, 27*(6), 12–25.

Bass, R. (1999). The scholarship of teaching: What's the problem? *Inventio, 1*(1). Retrieved December 15, 2008, from http://www.doiiit.gmu.edu/Archives/feb98/randybass.htm

Harding, S. (Ed.) (2004). Introduction: Standpoint theory as a site of political, philosophic, and scientific debate. In S. Harding (Ed.), *The feminist standpoint theory reader: Intellectual and political controversies* (pp. 1–16). New York: Routledge.

Hutchings, P. (2000). Introduction. In P. Hutchings (Ed.), *Opening lines: Approaches to the scholarship of teaching and learning* (pp. 1–10). Menlo Park, CA: The Carnegie Foundation for the Advancement of Teaching.

Mihans, R., Long, D., & Felten, P. (2008). Power and expertise: Student-faculty collaboration in course design and the scholarship of teaching and learning. *International Journal for the Scholarship of Teaching and Learning, 2*(2). Retrieved September 20, 2008, from http://academics.georgiasouthern.edu/ijsotl/v2n2/essays_about_esotl/PDFs/Essay_Felten_et_al.pdf

Pace, D. (2004). The amateur in the operating room: History and the scholarship of teaching and learning. *American Historical Review, 109*(4), 1171–1192.

Savory, P., Burnett, A. N., & Goodburn, A. (2007). *Inquiry into the college classroom: A journey toward scholarly teaching.* Bolton, MA: Anker.

Schulman, S., Bright, C., Duggins, K., Flannery, K., & McGarry, C. (2008). Student/faculty partnerships in course re-design: Learning about who students are to transform them. *Bridges: An Interdisciplinary Journal of Theology, Philosophy, History and Science, 15*(1/2), 181–204.

Shulman, L. (2000). From Minsk to Pinsk: Why a scholarship of teaching and learning? *Journal of Scholarship of Teaching and Learning, 1*(1), 48–53.

Weimer, M. (2006). *Enhancing scholarly work on teaching and learning: Professional literature that makes a difference.* San Francisco: Jossey-Bass.

2

STUDENTS IN PARLOR TALK ON TEACHING AND LEARNING

Conversational Scholarship

Carmen Werder, Luke Ware, Cora Thomas, and Erik Skogsberg

Imagine that you enter a parlor. You come late. When you arrive, others have long preceded you, and they are engaged in a heated discussion. . . . You listen for a while, until you decide that you have caught the tenor of the argument; then you put in your oar.

(Burke, 1941, p. 110)

We co-authors have participated in a special kind of parlor talk in Western Washington University's (WWU) Teaching-Learning Academy (TLA).[1] Our TLA is a dialogue forum for studying and strengthening the learning culture at WWU, which includes faculty, staff, alumni, and students from across campus. But unlike the argumentative exchange that Burke describes, we invite all participants to enter into a reasoned dialogue as they *put in their oars*. While Burke's phrase might suggest a situation where people "meddle or interfere" in matters that don't concern them, we use it deliberately to emphasize the absolute need for inviting students into a dialogue on teaching and learning. We need their expertise and guidance. Because we want to convey a sense of what we mean by *parlor talk*, we will try to replicate a similar kind of dialogue here. First, I, Carmen (TLA director and faculty in communication), will address my comments to Luke (a communication alumnus) who will respond and then address Cora (a communication alumna) who will answer and then address Erik (an English alumnus) who will respond to all. We invite you the readers to listen in (and sure, put in your oars along the way.)

CARMEN

Luke, I really miss seeing you in TLA. In fact I think of you each time we open the giant bag of pretzels before each dialogue group. I think of you sitting in the Fireplace Room judiciously munching pretzels until you were ready to speak.[2] I think of how expertly you helped launch the notion of an online forum, a virtual dialogue space designed to parallel TLA's real-time space—an idea that has now become a reality at WWU. In the online forum's advisory board meetings, I hear your voice cautioning us to "remember that it needs to have student buy-in, that it needs to be student driven; don't let the techies take it over." You were the first one I heard talk about the forum idea, you created a prototype, you were the one who inspired me and others to make it happen. You led the way.

But you were often willing to let me lead sometimes too. When we worked together in the communication course on dialogue (Civil Discourse as Interactive Learning) and you first began participating in the TLA as part of that course, I remember how keen you were on the theoretical tenets of dialogue. You understood straightaway the key distinction between *discussion* and *dialogue*. As you know, Ellinor and Gerard (1998) draw this distinction in terms of purpose: While discussion has a primary goal of convergence (reaching the best solution or answer), dialogue has a primary goal of divergence—exchanging a broad range of perspectives to achieve a deeper understanding. Divergence has proved so useful in opening up the space for student perspectives in the TLA conversation where deeper understanding of relationships between teaching and learning is the primary goal. That's why our TLA parlor is different from the one Burke suggests where discussion and arguing for the one best view seems the goal. Instead, we enter into a dialogue where understanding others' views (and our own) is the main goal.

I was particularly gratified the first time I heard you use the term *conversational scholarship*, a phrase that I had coined to describe the scholarship of teaching and learning (SoTL) model that I think TLA reflects. This dialogue model relies on constructing an intellectual space that invites students to participate as co-inquirers in investigating teaching and learning questions using an oral research approach. As a research model, it includes all the traditional inquiry steps associated with written scholarship: posing a question, collecting and analyzing data, formulating findings, and sharing results. But unlike the usual academic inquiry model, it pushes against the traditional boundaries of power and privilege that typically exclude students.

Conversational Scholarship Principles

I am grateful to you, Luke, for working with me to formulate five overarching principles for enacting this conversational scholarship model:

1. Create structured informality.

By formalizing the TLA dialogue with conversational agreements,[3] course credit for student participants, a shared research question, opening surveys, scribed dialogue group notes, and highlights of each dialogue round distributed through the Listserv, we have created a structure that echoes the traditional inquiry process.

2. Provide for shared ownership.

Because TLA members work collectively to identify a research question of shared interest to explore for 1 full academic year, participants feel more invested in the study.

3. Ensure reciprocal benefits.

Many faculty participants say they are surprised by how much students care about their learning, and as a result they feel more enthused about teaching them. Many also report changes in their teaching practices as a result of student comments made in TLA. Administrators have also identified benefits in terms of institutional change initiatives. Perhaps best of all, students report improved attitudes about faculty and staff that translate into better learning practices, such as taking advantage of office hours and asking more questions in class.

4. Invite broad-based and proportional representation.

The alliance TLA has built with a 100-level education course has ensured the ongoing inclusion of 1st-year students. And the civil discourse class, as well as offering communication practicum credit, has attracted a broad range of students from multiple majors. Since participants often invite their friends and colleagues to join the dialogue, we draw from most colleges and departments across the university, with many returning participants.

5. Recognize individual and collective expertise and contributions.

We make sure that the written TLA highlights feature collective insights as well as individual contributions.[4] Our annual spring Academy Awards ceremony, with its awards for individual and group recipients (from inside and outside TLA), has gone a long way to recognize contributions to teaching and learning far and wide.

Interestingly, these conversational scholarship principles parallel the qualities of participatory action research (PAR) that Otis and Hammond discuss in chapter 3. Both models provide strong theoretical foundations for student voices in SoTL, only from different disciplinary perspectives. While we use the TLA as a case study to suggest a new theoretical base for SoTL (i.e., conversational scholarship), Otis and Hammond use the TLA as an exemplum to connect an existing theoretical model to SoTL (i.e., PAR).

Embodied Scholarship

Luke, while you did not attend the 2006 International Society for the Scholarship of Teaching and Learning Conference in Washington, DC, perhaps you will recall the story that I told you about the tour guide I met at the National Museum of the American Indian. Not only was the tour guide a scholar, but he also embodied his scholarship in the way that he talked with us as we toured the exhibits. He brought not only his expertise but also a conversational style and respectful tone of voice that engaged my head and heart. During the tour, he frequently invited the group of thirty or so to respond with our observations and especially our questions. Often a question from us prompted his commentary, and he expressed genuine interest in our comments. Throughout I felt as if I were part of a co-inquiry walk/talk. When our tour ended, I went up to offer my appreciation. After thanking me, he pulled out a small journal that he was keeping and asked if I would please write down a few words describing my experience at the museum. Not only had he modeled the steps of scholarly inquiry in the tour conversation, but he also invited me to continue the dialogue. I felt honored that he wanted to keep the conversation going.

Pedagogy of Dialogue

In promoting a similar oral, embodied version of scholarship, it occurs to me that I am advocating for a signature pedagogy from my own discipline, that is, a pedagogy of dialogue. As Lee Shulman (2004) first observed, and Garung, Chick, and Haynie (2009) have elaborated on, we have signature pedagogies, or distinctive disciplinary ways of teaching and learning, and we would do well to understand them. In this case, I would urge anyone interested in bringing students squarely into the study of teaching and learning to tap into this rich pedagogy of dialogue coming out of communication studies.

Why is this embodied scholarship or pedagogy of dialogue so important? Mary Taylor Huber and Pat Hutchings (2005) point to its importance when they call for "more and better occasions to *talk* about learning" [emphasis mine] and when they propose that "students need to be part of the discussion" (pp. 118–119). I heartily agree that we need students but would add that we want *a broad range* of students and not only the high achieving ones or only the ones who voice their views in traditional leadership roles such as in student government. While undergraduate research efforts are vigorous in many institutions, those efforts necessarily can only engage a relatively small number of our students. And often these initiatives engage only those students who are already doing well—students who already know how to connect with faculty mentors, students who are already being heard. These initiatives frequently do not tap into the expertise of those learners who have not been successful in our institutions—learners whose views we ought to understand better. But if we want to tap into the latent expertise that all our students have about themselves as learners, we need parlor talk. So, Luke, what do you say?

Luke

Carmen, one of the strongest memories I have about TLA involves the first time I met you. We met at your office after a few days of back-and-forth e-mails where I begged you to let me into your class. Walking into your office, I remember seeing lots of chairs and a central coffee table where I found you sitting with Erik Skogsberg, one of our co-authors, in deep conversation about writing. The room had high ceilings and a real parlor feel to it. When we sat down to talk, we sat at a small circular table to discuss the course. You told me about the TLA and asked if I would be interested in joining that conversation. Before deciding, I paused to consider what exactly I was getting myself into. The course sounded unusual and different. Just your office alone, Carmen, was intimidating, located in one of the oldest buildings on campus that housed the highest administrators. Observing the floor-to-ceiling windows, I thought, you must be a real player in the higher-ed game, and I worried that you might be more engaged than I was ready to be. You clearly took academia very seriously, I suspected, and I wondered if that would hurt my grade.

Now, 3 years later, I laugh at that first memory. Since then you've moved your office more than once, a fact that reflects the whole idea of conversational scholarship—always evolving, always on the move. It turns out that the parlor outside your office and that round table next to your desk were much more important to you than the floor-to-ceiling windows. No matter where you go, you turn your spaces into environments where students can feel comfortable and feel part of the conversation.

I like that, even here discussing the need for students in any conversation about teaching and learning, you mention the idea of *broad-based representation*. A related memory sticks out for me from our trip to Douglas College in Vancouver, British Columbia, where we went to speak about conversational scholarship and the TLA. While discussing the need to include students, one of our hosts kindly proclaimed that I was a *keener* and that it was hard for them to get *nonkeener* students involved. A keener, we learned, meant a student who had always excelled academically. While I certainly enjoyed the sentiment, I had to protest the authenticity of using that word to describe me. I graduated from high school with a GPA below 2.0; I was hardly a keener in the traditional sense. The one class I got top marks in was clay design; I made the most inquisitive owl enjoyed by my mother to this day. Besides that single triumph, it wasn't until my 12th grade English class that I started to become keen on learning. Instead of opening in the usual, distanced fashion, my teacher took a different approach. He started off by telling us where he had been, what he had done, and why he was standing in front of us. He asked us to consider why we were sitting there with him too. I tried my hardest in that class and produced some of the best work he'd seen and I'd done.

In that experience, my teacher honored the metaphor that you, Carmen, believe we should honor: the idea of rowing a boat together. If all sides are not represented, then we'll likely end up rowing in circles. We agree with Burke (1941) that when we enter into scholarship, we enter into a conversation that has already begun and continues after we leave. To thrive, though, that conversation needs to include more voices; more people need seats at the table or in the boat with a chance to put in their oars. When it comes to teaching and learning, the only way the conversation can genuinely advance the scholarship is when student voices are present and heard. We have met countless people from institutions across many countries doing great things but are often missing crucial student perspectives. Being in my high school English class really gave me a chance to understand educators at a much deeper level. Then when I entered our TLA parlor for my first session, I began to understand myself as a learner. I realized that my voice was the missing piece in my own education.

At my first day in the TLA, I sat down in a high-backed parlor chair across from the fireplace. I sat with students, faculty, and staff about to engage in a completely new experience. The sense of excitement and intrigue was almost overwhelming. I also sat down next to important people who were much higher on the academic rungs—this chair was my first seat at the table. I felt anxious but compelled. We all sat quietly after the introductions, not really sure how to go forward. Finally the silence was broken; someone put a bowl of pretzels on our table, and the only returning member in our group jumped at them. Another professor in our group confessed he'd skipped lunch and was starving. I laughed and realized that professors were indeed human beings too. I scooped up some pretzels, and the conversation took off. To this day, I find it remarkable how effective pretzels are at disarming power differences between people.

As a communication major, I became fascinated with the TLA as a communication model, especially in the way it emphasizes dialogue—with the goal of shared understanding—and tries to include as many perspectives as possible. Trying to get students, faculty, and staff to meet that goal is a challenge. Through experience and collaborative research, I've found some key elements for why I believe the TLA has been so effective at elevating my student voice.

Own the Agenda

In the TLA everyone owns the agenda together. We each contribute to what we want the overarching research question to be. By building the question together from the ground up, students are on an equal footing with everyone else. TLA participants also create ground rules together to help ensure that professors don't fall into lecture mode. Students also serve as dialogue facilitators to ensure that everyone who wants to talk gets the chance. Ground rules and student facilitation are great ways to amplify the student voice.

Get Your Ducks Out of Rows

Meeting outside the typical classroom setting gives participants a chance to get some distance from engrained power boundaries. Stepping into a separate space enables us to redefine the dynamics within it more easily. Another important part of the TLA is that the space enables us to break up into smaller groups, circling our chairs so that we can see and hear each other clearly. In many classrooms chairs are bolted to the floor in rows. I know I'm right in thinking that looking at the back of a person's head all day doesn't exactly aid in meaningful conversation and learning.

Find the Voices

If you truly want to explore SoTL, you must ensure that all the voices are there. In TLA we welcome students, faculty, and staff from across campus (and even community members) because they are all key players in education. The notion that only the best and the brightest will want to engage in dialogue about teaching and learning is a myth. We can all become keeners; we just need to be invited. I have my high school and college report cards to prove it. Right now I'm really only an expert in one area: my own learning. I spent many years with little voice in my education, but now thanks to TLA I've had many years with an enormous voice.

Even if institutions can't afford the time or money to honor student voices in the way my institution does, I don't believe SoTL's efforts will be successful unless the schools take hold of some of these ideas. This dialogue has been a vital part of my experience in higher education. By sitting down and talking, I've learned a great deal about educators. Even more significantly, I've come to understand myself as a learner. I think these are goals we should all be striving for. And after all, are pretzels really that expensive?

In the TLA I didn't just develop a strong relationship with Carmen. I also had the chance to meet and work with a number of other students, including Cora Thomas with whom I did collaborative research. So, Cora, what did you find out?

CORA

Well, Luke, as you may remember, I really wanted to find out why students like me kept coming back to TLA, even when they weren't receiving credit for it. Here are a few things from my research of TLA that students have said about why they returned to TLA for multiple quarters:

- It's a space that lets me be open and honest with faculty and staff.
- I love the chance to talk, learn and develop relationships.
- Through dialogue we can start to understand each other's viewpoints about how we perceive our teaching and learning.
- As a student I [now] feel more involved in Western.
- The chance to listen to others' stories and ideas made me feel like I wasn't alone.

These individuals are not only conveying their reason for returning to the TLA, they are describing how this dialogue improved their learning experience. After collaboratively researching the TLA with you and others, I now understand that many students returned to the TLA for the same reason I did. It supported and encouraged my true passion for learning, a passion that has shaped my direction well beyond college.

As an individual who excelled in school my entire life (a contrast to your experience it seems, Luke), I was not surprised to find myself discovering the TLA. Like you, I didn't know what to expect, but I had a feeling it would be stimulating because of my prior experience in Carmen's rhetoric class where dialogue was central. And when I attended my first TLA gathering, I could see the environment was conducive to dialogue and sharing ideas. Not only did I participate in TLA for many quarters beginning in spring 2007, I was fortunate to begin collaborative research on the TLA itself.

As Carmen mentions earlier, it's rare for students to have the chance to become co-inquirers from the beginning of a project. Fortunately, that was our experience with our collaborative project. Carmen advised that 5 years worth of TLA data existed and was ripe for analysis. She never told us what to study; instead she asked our group to design a project together from square one. She and our student research team met to discuss the project and brainstorm research questions based on our individual interests. My interest was in motivation and my own intrinsic drive to obtain a full experience from my education. Jack Frymier (1970) describes the internal dimension of his academic motivation model saying, "some students seem to draw most heavily upon forces located within themselves to enhance their learning" (p. 28). Individual value systems represent a component of that internal dimension. Or, as Frymier puts it, "They believe in learning and knowledge" (p. 28). I had a hunch that my own attraction to TLA had to do with this belief. So I decided to focus my study on student motivation, that is, What motivates students to return to TLA for more than one quarter?

Working as part of a collaborative research team sharing data and insights, I focused my attention on student participants' expressed motives for continuing their participation. After suggesting that the opening TLA survey include a question about returning students, I analyzed the resulting data, including surveys, dialogue meeting highlights, and other artifacts. I used content analysis to examine student responses to the survey question, Have you participated in the TLA for more than this quarter? If yes, what made you come back? While it was a small sample group (only 24 *returning* student responses), it is significant that that many students returned to TLA in one quarter. And this feedback gave enormous insight into what keeps students coming back to the TLA and lays the groundwork for continued study.

What I found, Luke, is that participants' regard for the dialogue was the number one reason they continued to participate. So the data confirms what Carmen suggests in saying that it was the conversation itself that was so important. Their responses also suggest that the particular dialogue structure of the TLA (what we call *structured informality*) provided a sense of community, both intellectual and emotional.

Sometimes students characterized the attraction as *interaction,* saying they appreciated the chance to interact with professors and administrators. Students said they valued dialogue situated outside the classroom that acts as an "equal playing field" to voice concerns. One response describes this appreciation for a sense of equality: "I have realized how much I enjoy talking with staff members and administrators on this equal playing field." This response suggests TLA lowers the hierarchal walls of professor and student allowing them to relate as learners, studying together.

Some students described their motivation to participate in terms of *involvement* and a desire to make a difference in their institution and in their own education. In fact, many seem to be actively searching for involvement and the desire to make a difference, as reflected in this student's response:

"TLA is exactly what I've been looking for at Western." This suggests that students are seeking spaces to voice concerns about their own learning and are searching for places where they can be a part of a larger collective. As you and Carmen emphasize, and the data confirm: TLA not only benefits successful students, but it also serves the nonkeeners because it is the cross talk, the dialogue itself, that privileges and benefits all perspectives.

Students also pointed to the importance of TLA as a safe place, or as one student termed it, "a space that gives [me as a student] the opportunity to be open and honest with faculty and staff. Hard thing to come by as a student." The last comment is crucial in understanding how students often perceive traditional classrooms as less than conducive to genuine dialogue. They are looking for spaces where the traditional power dynamics of professor/student crumble away, a place like TLA where we can leave our official titles and rigid roles behind us.

In detailing why the dialogue was important to them, many TLA participants said they returned because of the director who also served as the overall facilitator. You and I are not surprised by this finding because we have returned to TLA in great part because of Carmen. Leaders' personal characteristics, the values they hold, and the extent of their commitment contribute to how others perceive the organization. If Carmen had not demonstrated the same principles as the organization, its student participants may not have been so eager to return. In this case, it was her facilitative ability—her ability to model facilitated dialogue—that proved to be perhaps the most positive influence on these students. Frymier (1970) states, "What teachers say, how they say it and the values which they reflect in their daily teaching all become perceivable substances from the learner's point of view. They are the feedback which students use to build their own conceptions of self" (p. 31). Carmen's positive aura and interest in ensuring that everyone has ample air time promotes an optimistic student reaction and builds students' self-esteem.

Through examining this student feedback, I understand how important it is for Western, and perhaps for every institution, to have a space for students to connect with others very different from themselves, to encounter different viewpoints and experiences, and to combine all their innovative ideas to improve the learning environment. I believe that faculty, staff, and administrators *need* to hear from students, keeners and nonkeeners as well as in-betweeners, because they have expertise to share and they need a place to voice it. Students are returning to TLA because this organization provides what they are searching for: a venue to voice their insights about teaching and learning, and a privileged place in an intellectual and social community that needs them.

Being a member of the TLA and a student of it, I worked as a participant observer. I knew my own motivations for returning and wondered if other students would have different reasons. After completing my study, I realized their motivations paralleled my own. Now, I wonder if the relationships forged in the TLA dialogue have changed their life, viewpoints, and reiterated values, the same way this experience has affected me.

My choice to join the TLA was the smartest decision I made while attending Western. Thank you for steering me in the right direction, Luke. Now that I've put in my oar, Erik, will you tell us about your journey in these teaching and learning waters?

ERIK

Thank you, Cora. I'm a few years past my experience in the TLA and—because of the passion for education developed there—I've finished a master's in teaching program. I find myself in an interesting position as I now try to make sense of the teaching and learning landscape from a different position: my 1st year teaching English at a rural public high school in Washington State.

Early this school year, I rushed into one of my American literature classes to scrawl a journal prompt on the board. Students were spilling in behind me, buzzing with noise, trying to catch the last couple of minutes of talk before the bell rang. As I finished at the board, I caught the tenor of one student's conversation about a pop song. Nonchalantly, I made a joke using the artist's name, and the student immediately stopped his conversation to address me in surprised shock at the fact that I knew about the music he listened to. The group of students he had been talking to were also now staring expectantly. Questions then began flooding in as students pried me for information about the types of music I listened to and artists I liked. Not soon after, the questions turned to my experience in high school, why I chose to teach, where I've traveled, and how I proposed to my wife. I rattled off a few artists' names in response to the first student's question—startled that this topic would win the students' interest and the connection to my class I had been hoping for. A bit impatient with this exchange, I pushed forward. Students raised their hands. More questions. All personal.

Seeing that none of the questions connected directly to the lesson I planned for the day, I begrudgingly decided to let them continue; at least the students were engaged, they were actually listening to each other's questions and to my answers. What had on previous days been a difficult attempt by me to get them interested in the subject of early American literature now gave way to the classroom I wanted: student engagement, connection with each other, readiness to ask questions. And everything seemed effortless. We were connecting. They loved it. I loved it. But I didn't want to be the young 1st-year teacher who wins over students by just talking to them about their favorite music, letting them co-opt classroom time and space for a conversation they could just as easily have with friends. I didn't want to be that young teacher who eased the difficulties inherent in the 1st year of teaching by being friends with the students. However, I couldn't deny how well everything had gone in that short period of time, and after we got back to the journal prompt, students seemed more willing to work with me.

Later that week I stayed after school with a group of students from that class and approached them about what happened earlier. What did they get out of it? Students responded candidly about how they didn't feel connected with some of their teachers but wanted to. They said that by knowing things about me—things I initially saw as trivial, like what music I listened to—they were better able to relate me. And, as a result of this connection, they wanted to do the work. Being so focused on covering my lessons in the previous weeks, I had missed this simple formula: Pay attention to who my students are as people, and they will pay more attention to me and their learning. Allow all of us to share who we are outside the classroom and we can connect better inside, making for a better learning experience—for all of us. I had been so connected to subject and institution that I had forgotten to connect to the students in my classroom. I learned what Luke's high school English teacher apparently knew: Teaching and learning are relational activities. We must be in relationship with each other for learning to happen.[5]

I see that instance as a turning point for me this year. It marked the realization that up until that moment, what I had so valued about my educational experience through the TLA, had been absent in my own classroom. I found that despite all my work in SoTL, despite all the conversations I had with faculty and students in TLA, and despite all I had advocated for in terms of liberatory pedagogy and democratic educational systems when in college, I was letting the subject and the institution drive my work.

After these conversations with my students, I have begun to refocus my attention on creating a space in my classroom where they can talk about their own learning, and where I'm conscious of how my material connects with my students. Now I feel we're not solely focused on either the subject or on talking about pop music but somewhere in the middle—balancing an awareness of self, subject, and student. And while I can't say that I always succeed in achieving this balancing, I can say that at least I'm clearer now on the potential of this pedagogical stance, am reinvested in the value it can have for any educational environment, and I believe I can look to my students to help lead the way. I'm also reminded of a realization I made through TLA conversation. The best classrooms are not teacher or learner centered but *learning centered*, and to convene at this point we must dance around it through human connection, dialogue, and relationship. Unfortunately traditional academic structures don't naturally create space for this type of conversation, so we—as in the TLA—need to deliberately carve out institutional space for connection and divergent dialogue.

As we have tried to show in this chapter, it takes a deliberate decentering of traditional structures—including models of scholarship—to create this dialogical relationship. We must shy away from worn-out structures that don't give us the necessary means of connection and dialogue we so desperately need. We also must be cautious of falling into old patterns under the guise of SoTL work. Every time we limit voices in the conversation about teaching and learning, we're continuing the outdated model of undemocratic academic inquiry. We must be wary of only allowing students into SoTL conversation in an effort to simply inform them how teaching and learning works. While students have much to gain from teachers in a SoTL exchange, faculty and institutions have just as much to gain from the students about how learning works. If this reciprocity doesn't happen, what results is a monologue about teaching and learning.

The SoTL conversation is not complete without what Hutchings (2005) has called a student's *pedagogical intelligence*. And while I agree with Hutchings that it's important to "[raise] the quality of feedback [students] can offer" (para. 4) by making them more aware of their own learning, I would also caution us not to risk pushing for what we see as more informed feedback at the expense of genuine feedback from our students. We need to hear what students really are thinking even when, perhaps especially when, it does not match what we assume. We also need to make sure that we communicate to our students that they are not meddlers, but valued contributors in our parlor talk about teaching and learning. But, of course, we must first believe that they really are essential to the conversation, to the scholarship. What will emerge is a setting that fosters connection for genuine real-time SoTL to occur and to create an environment that values education as a democratic enterprise.

So I'm not surprised that in hearing from all of you, the theme that continually comes up is connection: Carmen, your apt metaphor of a new kind of academic parlor reinvigorated by what you term *conversational scholarship*; Luke, your realization—through pretzels—of the humanity we all share; and, Cora, your findings on the importance of dialogue as a motivating force for engaged learning. It was this same kind of intellectual and human connection that my students helped me remember. On that day I was so busy focusing on my subject and filling an institutional role that I had forgotten them. SoTL has the potential to reconnect faculty, staff, students, and administrators with each other, with themselves, with the institution, and as human beings. In the end I'm finding that despite all the usual bumps that come along with being a 1st-year teacher, my time working in SoTL via the TLA is helping me create a space in my own classroom where parlor talk is integral to learning. Then again, perhaps you should ask my students.

Notes

1. We are grateful for the role that the Carnegie Academy for the Scholarship of Teaching and Learning (CASTL) played in prompting the creation of our TLA as part of Western's response to the CASTL Campus Conversations Program. We thank the many students, faculty, staff, administrators, community members, and alumni who have entered the TLA parlor at WWU since its conception in 1999— those who have joined us for a short time, those who have stayed, and those who foster similar dialogue wherever they go. We appreciate the contributions that our critical friends from Elon (especially Christopher Manor, Stephen Bloch-Schulman, and Peter Felten) as well as from North Seattle Community College (Tom Drummond and Kalyn Owens) made as we composed this chapter.

2. The TLA meets in what's called the Canada House, former residence of the university president and now home to the Canadian-American Studies Program. TLA uses the whole first floor, which includes a room with a fireplace.

3. Students who participate in the TLA as a practicum for a civil discourse class help draft/revise the agreements used, and every quarter we ask all participants to endorse them/suggest revisions.

4. TLA meets every other week. When it doesn't meet, the TLA director sends out highlights of the previous week's dialogue based on group dialogue notes with the help of TLA student staff.

5. Erik would like to thank the students in his sixth period American literature class at Yelm High School for helping him—especially that day—be a better teacher.

References

Burke, K. (1941). *The philosophy of literary form: Studies in symbolic action* (3rd ed.). Berkeley: University of California Press.

Ellinor, L., & Gerard, G. (1998). *Dialogue: Rediscover the transforming power of conversation.* New York: Wiley.

Frymier, J. R. (1970). Motivation: The mainspring and gyroscope of learning. *Theory Into Practice, 9*(1), 23–32.

Garung, R. A., Chick, N. L., & Haynie, A. (Eds.). (2009). *Exploring signature pedagogies: Approaches to teaching disciplinary habits of mind.* Sterling, VA: Stylus.

Huber, M. T., & Hutchings, P. (2005). *The advancement of learning: Building the teaching commons.* San Francisco: Jossey-Bass.

Hutchings, P. (2005). Building pedagogical intelligence. *Carnegie Perspectives.* Retrieved January 31, 2009, from http://www.carnegiefoundation.org/perspec tives/sub.asp?key = 245& subkey = 571

Shulman, L. S. (2004, October). *In search of signature pedagogies: Learning from lessons of practice.* Paper presented at the International Society for the Scholarship of Teaching and Learning Conference, Bloomington, IN.

3

PARTICIPATORY ACTION RESEARCH AS A RATIONALE FOR STUDENT VOICES IN THE SCHOLARSHIP OF TEACHING AND LEARNING

Megan M. Otis and Joyce D. Hammond

T he growing number of institutions in higher education where students are actively entering into the scholarship of teaching and learning (SoTL) attests to a powerful paradigm shift in which students are recognized and supported as important partners in understanding and improving teaching and learning.[1] Yet, for some professionals in higher education, the idea of including students as co-researchers in SoTL represents a radical concept that runs counter to the historical model of education in which faculty disseminate information to students who pay for the privilege of receiving their teachers' accumulated knowledge. Even at colleges and universities that welcome students into arenas of examination and praxis within SoTL, professionals often find themselves on the defensive, scrambling to explain to skeptics why students' opinions, experiences, and suggestions are vital when studying how best to learn and teach.

In this chapter, we offer participatory action research (PAR) as a valuable alternative to other research approaches for SoTL, because it provides a methodological rationale for including students as co-researchers. PAR supports the inclusion of students' *insider* knowledge of their expertise as learners. PAR also calls for the construction of new knowledge that arises when *all* stakeholders, including students, collaborate in inquiry processes leading to positive changes in education. As applied to SoTL, PAR not only recognizes the value of student input, it calls for its absolute necessity.

The Carnegie Academy for the Scholarship of Teaching and Learning (CASTL) has recognized Western Washington University (WWU) as an institutional leader for student voices in SoTL based on the work of our Teaching-Learning Academy (TLA). A forum that includes faculty, staff, administrators, community members, and students, the TLA works to deepen individual understanding of teaching and learning through dialogue and to strengthen the educational culture through collective action. The TLA exemplifies PAR in many ways, especially in its inclusion of student voices. To explain WWU's PAR-SoTL model, we will begin by describing PAR as a research method and methodology. We briefly discuss contemporary uses of PAR in education. We then examine our TLA as a PAR-SoTL case study and detail seven significant ways it incorporates PAR principles. Finally, drawing upon our anthropological training, we reflect upon our participant observation in the TLA, describe the process of coming to the realization that our SoTL work in the TLA is a PAR process, and share the profound impact of our new collective knowledge made possible by the inclusion of student voices.

PAR

PAR is a qualitative, cyclical research process that differs significantly from quantitative, hypothesis-testing, positivist research done by *experts* on *subjects*. In PAR the subjects themselves become researchers. As participant researchers, people draw upon their understandings of personal and social realities to construct new group knowledge. Together they identify pertinent questions that lead to effective planning and action to create change that is meaningful to *them*. As PAR practitioners reflect on their research results and consider the outcome of actions based on their findings, they enter another cycle of PAR to reexamine or create new questions that in turn lead to further research, reflection, and action.

While many diagrams of the PAR process exist (e.g., Kemmis & McTaggart, 2005, p. 564; Stringer, 2007, p. 9), McIntyre's (2008) drawing, "The Recursive Process of PAR" (see Figure 3.1), clearly illustrates the recursive process of PAR that involves "questioning a particular issue; reflecting upon

FIGURE 3.1
The Recursive Process of PAR

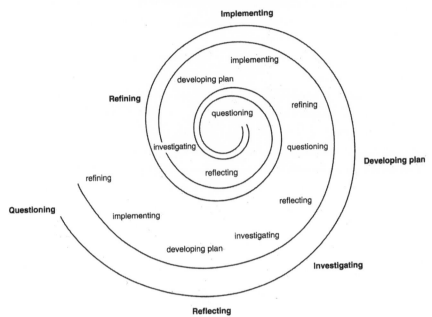

Note: From *Participatory Action Research*, by A. McIntyre, 2008, Thousand Oaks, CA, Sage, p. 7. Copyright 2008 by Sage Publications. Reprinted with permission.

and investigating the issue; developing an action plan; [and] implementing and refining said plan" (p. 7). While any linear illustration of the PAR process inadequately illustrates its reiterative nature, many circular models over-simplify the process. McIntyre's diagram "represents how various aspects of the PAR process are fluidly braided within one another in a spiral of reflection, investigation and action" (p. 6). Each phase of the PAR cycle includes all features of the process, thus ensuring the benefits of PAR methodology at each stage of a project.

Initially PAR was developed in reaction to criticisms of positivist methodology. First effectively used in developing countries, PAR flourished during the 1960s and 1970s and is now used worldwide in a variety of contexts (for in-depth information on the history of PAR, see Bradbury & Reason, 2001; Fine et al., 2004; Greenwood & Levin, 2007; Kemmis & McTaggart, 2005). PAR is a form of critical social science methodology that challenges the notion that only evidence resulting from experimentation is valid (Neuman, 1997). The paradigm shift that PAR and other action research methodologies offer often prompts skepticism and resistance. Although scholars have effectively addressed criticisms of validity, replicability, and other primarily quantifiable standards (Bradbury & Reason, 2001; Kemmis & McTaggart, 2005), it is noteworthy that fundamentally criticisms of PAR and other action research approaches result from the prevalent attitude that only experts and authorities are qualified to undertake research and initiate change. Research and planned actions undertaken by "ordinary" people may be considered suspect as a result of positivist attitudes that hold that real research must be disengaged and objective. However, it is precisely *because* stakeholders' research questions and motives link to what matters to a group of people that PAR is a powerful approach for studying and instigating change. As many feminist, collaborative, community-based, and critical researchers have been pointing out for the past few decades, much traditional research never benefited its subjects (e.g., Ezzy, 2002; Reason & Bradbury, 2006; Stoecker, 2005). Even when researchers have sought insiders' perspectives to create an agenda of change, many of the planned projects have failed since the participants had no investment in the projects that would motivate them to pursue the resulting recommendations. With PAR, stakeholders own all aspects and outcomes of the research process.

Today, as Alice McIntyre (2008) points out, "Practitioners of PAR engage in a variety of research projects, in a variety of contexts, using a wide range of research practices that are related to an equally wide range of political ideologies" (p. 1). The similarities underlying such diverse work are connected with the double objective that informs all PAR projects: to produce knowledge and action directly useful to a community (through research, education, and sociopolitical action) and the goal of *consciousness-raising*. Consciousness-raising is a process by which people construct and use their *own* knowledge to understand the established power structures, to see how those in power have created and used knowledge production for their own benefit (Reason, 1994). PAR places emphasis on work that is practical, critical, and emancipatory. PAR practitioners also share the goal of using their research to create change in practices, attitudes, and policies to create more positive outcomes.

While many fields have used PAR, including anthropology, sociology, community health, and medicine, education is one arena in which PAR and other action research approaches have been flourishing. Some teachers involve their students in disciplinary-based PAR projects, inside and outside school (e.g., Ozer et al., 2008; Stewart, Riecken, Scott, Tanaka, & Riecken, 2008). Also, many teachers undertake action research to study and improve their own pedagogy; in fact those who believe that the goal of SoTL is to improve teaching and learning have argued that all SoTL *is* action research (e.g., Schön, 1995).

PAR and Student Voices

While all SoTL may be action research, for SoTL to be *participatory* action research, it must be done in collaboration with all stakeholders, including and especially students. Based on the PAR premise that those with a stake in a situation are most qualified to exchange knowledge and future visions with other stakeholders, it follows conceptually and ethically that students should participate in decisions that will directly affect their life. As primary stakeholders of their education, students should rightfully take their place alongside faculty, administrators, and staff in researching, planning, and implementing actions that best serve their educational needs. Although educators are ever more attuned to "student-centered learning" in the management of classrooms, the creation of assignments, and the facilitation of internships, research projects, and other learning opportunities, many educators and other higher education professionals have not consciously considered the practical, critical, and innovative dimensions of including students as stakeholders in SoTL research.

SoTL inquiry projects are ideal for setting PAR projects in motion. By collaborating, stakeholders in an educational institution can investigate educational practices and their consequences, study the societal conditions that shape individuals' and institutional realities, plan and launch changes that will contribute to better outcomes, and evaluate and reflect on what to retain, what to reexamine, and what to change in a new cycle. Not only do all parties learn more about each other's issues, concerns, hopes, and difficulties—resulting in all of them becoming better informed and more knowledgeable about those they interact with in a variety of ways—at the same time, they build a foundation of honoring one another's contributions and strengthen an institution's democratizing message. PAR practices also enact other key values espoused by colleges and universities, such as respect for diversity in people and perspectives; engaged, interactive, and collaborative study; and strong communication skills.

Case Study: The TLA

The TLA is a forum for dialogue and action at WWU to promote SoTL. Currently the TLA has about 100 participants including students, faculty, staff, and administrators from many departments across the university, as well as a few community members and alumni. For the most part, members participate on a voluntary basis. However, some students do receive credit through several courses including a 300-level communication course, a 1st-year education class, and a practicum in applied communication. Participants meet in small groups of about 20 to 30 people on a biweekly basis throughout the academic year. Four different dialogue groups meet on different days and times to accommodate the participants' varied availability. The structure is flexible enough that participants can engage in a variety of different ways for periods of time ranging from one quarter to many years.

Each year TLA participants collectively develop one or more related research questions for self-study. In the inquiry phase, the paid staff members (including a director and a few student employees, most with work study programs) create an open-ended survey and administer it to all participants. The initial surveys probe participants' interests, helping them identify the issues and topics they feel would benefit from collective study and action. TLA staff members compile the survey data and detect patterns across the survey responses, identifying any emergent themes the whole group can use to construct one overarching research question. Through dialogue, TLA members frame the question and probe it further to discover more specific questions to examine over the course of the year. For example, the dominant question for the 2007–08 academic year was: "What keeps us from genuine dialogue, and what would encourage that dialogue in sustaining a respectful, inclusive learning culture?" Within that larger question, TLA members identified specific questions such as: "How can co-inquiry and co-mentoring positively shape teaching and learning?" and "What innovations in assessing teaching and learning can be utilized to encourage genuine dialogue between faculty and students?" Once TLA members collectively determine the principle research question and explore possible subquestions, the TLA staff clusters each dialogue group into mini dialogue groups based on the participants' identified interests.

The TLA's collaborative inquiry on teaching and learning relies primarily on dialogue and surveys, but other tools are also used, such as 3D visual models. Using different kinds of visual and kinesthetic tools prompts participants to think about teaching and learning in new ways. Such tools also encourage participants to interact with one another in different ways, allow creative expression of participants' diverse perspectives, and help to engage those with different learning styles.

As a result of dialogue on the questions, ideas for changes emerge, and by the second term of the year (though often sooner), the TLA shifts to planning and implementing action items. Participants bring their time and their talents to bear in different ways; not every TLA member directly participates in every action project or contributes in the same ways.

Change stemming from TLA dialogue transpires on many levels. Much change takes place on the micro level; individuals make changes to their own teaching and learning based on what they've heard in the TLA dialogue. For example, many students have noted that they now ask questions in class and seek out faculty during office hours. Sometimes change occurs at a program or department level. For instance, a department altered its tenure and promotion policies to reward participation in the TLA as service. Many changes also occur at the institutional or macro level; for example, in 2002 the TLA sent recommendations to the General Education Task Force that heavily influenced the reshaping of the general university requirements for all WWU undergraduates.

PAR Qualities of the TLA

Paralleling the qualities that distinguish PAR from other forms of research, the TLA is participatory, collaborative, democratizing, action oriented, and cyclical. Additionally, TLA staff members have a role similar to the role of the researcher-facilitator in PAR as discussed by Stringer (2007).

Participatory

So many different people (students, staff, faculty, administrators) from all around Western's campus (and even the wider community) are included in the TLA dialogue. Because so many different people participate, I get to hear lots of diverse ideas and I've learned to see teaching and learning in lots of different ways. (TLA student, personal communication, October 8, 2008)

The TLA is highly participatory because it is inclusive of *all* stakeholders in the teaching-learning process. While faculty of all ranks, and students, undergraduate and graduate, constitute the majority of the TLA participants, other stakeholders also participate in the TLA (although less prominently): staff members and administrators of varying ranks from student affairs and academic affairs, community members from off campus including local businesspeople, political leaders, parents, alumni, and educators from other institutions. No one is excluded from participating in the TLA; indeed, participants continually strive to be as inclusive as possible and often ask themselves, Who is not present in this dialogue who ought to be here? When participants identify voices that are missing in the dialogue, the TLA staff sends out special invitations to those individuals or groups.

As previously discussed, the research process includes all stakeholder-participants in each step of the research process: developing the research question, collecting data, analyzing data, planning, and carrying out action. When all stakeholders participate in each stage of the research, there is a greater sense of investment in the project that helps to sustain interest over time. The TLA has emphasized collectively developing a research question, typically devoting an entire academic quarter to this phase of research. Once a research question emerges, participants complete a survey stemming from the research question, which allows the group to tap into each participant's unique perspectives and experiential knowledge pertaining to the research question. This data collection simultaneously positions each TLA participant as researcher and research subject. During the course of the research, TLA participants may extend their inquiry to stakeholding groups outside the TLA; initially, however, the research starts with TLA participants themselves.

Collaborative

As a first year student at Western I felt like my only contribution to the school was to reach my own goals as an independent student. Once I got involved with TLA, I felt as though I was part of a community on campus, with a collective of individuals trying to reach goals that affected everyone at Western. (TLA student, personal communication, October 7, 2008)

According to Stringer (2007), action research "results not only in a collective vision but also in a sense of community" (p. 11). In collaborating, TLA members create new understandings about teaching and learning and spark action projects based on these new understandings; at the same time they create connections among themselves. Members of the campus community connect with others they may never interact with in the course of their typical work routines. The informal interactions in TLA are humanizing and offer faculty, students, and other stakeholders glimpses into the backstage areas of each other's life. Students often remark that they never realized how much their professors care about their teaching, and, conversely, faculty frequently comment that they never realized how deeply students care about their learning. Collaboration in TLA reinforces a common bond all the stakeholders share—a commitment to teaching and learning—which allows all participants to realize they are not isolated but part of a larger learning community.

Democratizing

> I really enjoyed getting to freely express my opinions to faculty and staff. In a classroom it can often feel as though students' opinions don't matter, and this was an opportunity to have my opinions heard. (TLA student, Closing Survey, winter 2007)

The TLA strives to create a space that values all participants equally and legitimizes individual knowledge on teaching and learning. Regardless of rank or position within the university, each stakeholder has expertise based on unique educational experiences. At the beginning of every term, participants agree to shared ground rules, which aid in ensuring equity among participants. In education, often marked by a strict hierarchy in which faculty do most of the talking while students listen and "store" faculty's knowledge, the TLA supports democratization in several ways. Students are able to voice their opinions to faculty, administrators, and staff members more openly, knowing their ideas won't be graded. The TLA model urges the breakdown of the barriers typically reinforced by a university power structure; titles are de-emphasized, and students facilitate the dialogue in small groups, a role typically filled by their professors.

Action Oriented

> For me, the real reward isn't the dialogue that takes place each TLA session (though the dialogue is rewarding; fun, too), it's the action that happens

because of it. The new online forum, the Student Voices club, the Festival of Scholarship; these evolved from thoughts expressed through collaborative dialogue. (TLA student, personal communication, October 8, 2008)

While the primary goal of TLA dialogue has always been to cultivate a deeper understanding of teaching and learning from multiple perspectives, acting on that new understanding to create positive changes in teaching and learning has also evolved as a major aim. When the TLA first formed, taking action was not originally one of its primary objectives. Over time, TLA participants—especially students—repeatedly voiced their interest and desire to *do something* with their newfound insights on teaching and learning. Planning and enacting action projects are now an integral part of each TLA research cycle.

Reaching beyond the inclusion of student voices in dialogue, students are also primary actors effecting change planned collectively by TLA members. Often students spearhead and carry out the action projects proposed within the TLA via follow-up independent study and practicum projects for credit. For example, during the 2007–08 academic year, a TLA student participant developed a proposal for a campuswide online dialogue forum as a way to cultivate genuine dialogue across multiple perspectives; TLA members, including other students, then created partnerships with staff and administrators from the library, as well as academic technology, to form an advisory board to create the online dialogue forum (launched in the fall of 2008, see http://forum.wwu.edu).

Cyclical

Coming up with the question for next quarter has been great. It has been neat to be a part of devising what people will be studying/reflecting on for next year. (TLA student, Closing Survey, spring 2006)

In 2008 Western began its 10th year of SoTL research and dialogue. Each year represents a cycle in a continuously evolving research spiral. Each cycle typically includes the development of a new research question, the exploration of that question through surveys and dialogue, and a period of planning and carrying out actions. Reflection is an ongoing part of each stage. At the end of each cycle, the participants "leave a legacy," some type of artifact that represents the new understandings created and the work accomplished. Such an act ensures that TLA participants in future cycles (as well as others outside the TLA) will benefit from past participants' experiences.

Celebration is also a very important part of each cycle. At the end of each academic year, the TLA hosts its Academy Awards ceremony and reception. TLA participants nominate individuals and groups they believe exemplify the various creative responses to the yearly research question. The goal of the ceremony is to recognize efforts widely; everyone nominated with an appropriate rationale receives an award. The Academy Awards showcases the TLA's research findings and action projects, recognizes and celebrates excellent and innovative contributions to teaching and learning from inside and outside the TLA, and recruits new participants.

TLA Staff as PAR Researcher-Facilitator

> We seemed to have great participation from students and faculty . . . due to the facilitators' great guidance. (TLA student, Closing Survey, spring 2006)

Ideally, PAR is a grassroots effort; typically, however, a researcher-facilitator serves as a catalyst to initiate or assist a group in the research process. While the researcher-facilitator plays a different role in the research process, the person is equivalent to other collaborators and is also a stakeholder. TLA staff members serve in the role of PAR researcher-facilitator. In addition to bringing their own knowledge of the educational system as faculty and students to TLA, the staff members also play the roles of catalyst, resource person, supporter, and facilitator. Additionally, the TLA staff assist the other participants in the research process by recording key ideas arising in the dialogue, compiling notes, highlighting emergent themes, and presenting the information to the group for further analysis as well as publishing and presenting findings more widely in national and international venues. The staff members reinforce and facilitate the collaborative process of the TLA without imposing direction or influencing the research outcomes.

PAR Outcomes for TLA Students

> I've learned I need to be an active learner, I felt passive this quarter/my whole educational career and [the TLA] brought it to my attention that it's my responsibility to take charge of my education. (TLA student, Closing Survey, spring 2003)

Based on some preliminary results of Megan's thesis research (Otis, 2010), the outcomes for students who participate in the TLA are similar to the outcomes for participants of other PAR projects. Students, typically silenced by the power structure of the traditional classroom, generally feel they are powerless to effect change and think they do not have a voice in how their classroom or school operates (e.g., TLA Opening Surveys, fall 2003). In participating in the TLA, they discover that their knowledge and understanding of teaching and learning is valuable and legitimate. Faculty, staff, and administrators in the TLA are very curious and eager to hear what students think and say about different aspects of teaching and learning. Students become more aware of the power dynamics at work in the university and their position within that power structure; awareness that Paulo Freire (1970/2000) refers to as *conscientization*, or consciousness-raising. TLA student participants are empowered by their experiences in TLA and transform from passive spectators to active participants in their own education and in the university community. Even if students encounter resistance or hesitancy outside the TLA, they often report being able to retain their awareness and increased sense of agency or self-efficacy.

Our Stakeholder Stories

As a graduate student and a faculty member who cumulatively share 16 years' engagement with the TLA and, simultaneously, as anthropologists, we see connections between our evolving discipline and our experiences with SoTL. Just as postmodern anthropology has increasingly questioned anthropologists' authoritative representations of others and recognized the co-construction of knowledge with cultural insiders (e.g., Fluehr-Lobban, 2008; Lassiter, 2005), so too has SoTL begun to co-create knowledge with students as researchers. Recognizing ourselves simultaneously as researchers and subjects of higher education, we draw upon our background experiences to reflexively share the development of our thinking about PAR and the SoTL work of TLA.

JOYCE'S STORY

Like others of my generation enrolled in graduate programs in the 1970s, I received very little training or support in learning how to teach. Research in the discipline was regarded as paramount to securing and keeping a faculty position. Despite the lack of any training in how to organize and teach classes, the anthropological mandate of "getting the native point of view" served me well in the long run. As "native" to the institutions of higher education, students' perspectives are not only important, they are at the heart of educational culture. If faculty, staff, and administrators truly are to serve students, they must take students' realities and needs into consideration. Welcoming students into the investigation of educational practices to improve education is equivalent to applied anthropological projects in which anthropologists create partnerships *with* people to achieve those changes that best reflect people's attitudes, concerns, and hopes for better futures.

When WWU joined CASTL, I and about 30 faculty from across the university came together to discuss learning and teaching. However, it was not until one faculty member asked, "Where are the students?" that we began to contemplate the significance of including or excluding students in SoTL. By working with students, WWU's TLA effectively communicates that students are indeed key stakeholders in higher education. Their perspectives, experiences, and visions are integral to our questions and understanding of teaching and learning.

As the TLA evolved to include students, faculty, staff, and administrators began to reap the benefits of gaining access to student ideas and opinions on various topics and issues. For me, the impact of student participation in the TLA has ranged from hearing students' creative ideas about TLA action projects to the effects of taking risks in collaborating with students in teaching, research, and publication projects. The courage to work with students in new ways, for example, led to my excitement and receptivity when two graduate students approached me about offering an applied course to follow a more traditional fieldwork methods course I taught. PAR came onto the horizon for all three of us at an applied anthropology conference; we then co-originated and co-taught the first PAR class at our university.

A few years later, Megan and I came to our own separate epiphanies that the TLA was a PAR project. Through our new PAR lens, we understood why the epistemological underpinnings of WWU's TLA, which included a commitment to including students' voices, were working so well. Our realization seemed, in retrospect, so apparent that we were amazed that we hadn't realized it before.

MEGAN'S STORY

My involvement with TLA and SoTL and my involvement with PAR have until recently seemed like two entirely separate entities in my college life; while not immediately apparent to me, connecting SoTL and PAR was like connecting two interlocking puzzle pieces to reveal a bigger picture. I came to WWU as an undergraduate student in the fall of 2001 from a high school in a Seattle suburb with about 1,400 students to a university with about 12,000 students. The shift to such a large institution from my much smaller high school was traumatic; I didn't know anyone and I felt lost. Carmen Werder, the director of the TLA, was assigned as my faculty adviser, so I made an appointment with her for advice on which classes to take. She recommended I take a course that she was teaching called Learning Reconsidered because I had expressed an interest in education. I did not know it at the time, but this course was my first introduction to SoTL. It was also part of WWU's involvement with CASTL. Learning Reconsidered was a transformative learning experience for me because it helped me to examine my approach to learning in different ways. I must have left an impression on Carmen as well because she called me up and offered me a job. I worked part-time for the TLA for 3 years until I graduated in 2005, and my experiences in the TLA drastically shaped my whole educational experience. I went from being lost in a sea of 12,000 students to part of a small learning community where I connected with faculty, administrators, staff members, and other students from around the campus, which really helped me to feel more comfortable and at home at WWU.

My involvement with TLA also connected me to WWU's involvement in the CASTL Student Voices group. I and several other students attended numerous conferences to co-present our research and specifically to represent how WWU was involving students in its SoTL work. I really had no idea how distinctive our work in TLA was until I tried to explain it to SoTL scholars from other institutions.

My involvement in TLA also heavily influenced my decision to become an anthropology major. Shortly after I began working for Carmen, I enrolled in an introductory course in cultural anthropology taught by Joyce. I had first met Joyce in TLA, so when I became a student in her class as a sophomore, I felt a bit more comfortable speaking up in class, asking questions, and seeking help during her office hours. I was able to interact with the material more deeply than I had in any other class before, and my positive learning experiences in that class inspired me to declare anthropology my major and also led me to enroll in many more courses with Joyce.

It wasn't until I came back to WWU for graduate school that I enrolled in Joyce's PAR class, and it was during that class one day when it hit me: *TLA is PAR!* It was one of those magical lightbulb moments that I imagine all faculty wish for their students, when suddenly the light of understanding dawns and you connect two things that previously seemed unrelated. I was so profoundly affected by my experience in that class, and especially by how it connected to my experiences in TLA with SoTL, that a year later I came back to the PAR class as a co-teacher, and it also led me to combine these two threads into my thesis research.

Conclusion

SoTL scholars need to reexamine how knowledge is created and whose knowledge is considered legitimate. Historically, *experts* in higher education have conducted research to create new knowledge. But PAR legitimizes *all* stakeholders' knowledge, and as a major stakeholder group, students become co-researchers in PAR. Students need to be part of SoTL, not only because of their sheer numbers but because there is so much at stake for them. In advocating for student voices in SoTL, we're not arguing that faculty and other stakeholders' experiences and expertise be diminished or suppressed. We *are* arguing that students' experiences and expertise be considered just as legitimate and necessary for a more complete picture of teaching and learning. Although length limitations of this chapter prevent us from exploring ways to apply PAR to SoTL in depth, any SoTL project incorporating PAR should start with a consideration of how students can act as research partners from start to finish.

As a model of inquiry, PAR is participatory, collaborative, democratizing, action oriented, and cyclical—all traits necessary for supporting students' contributions to SoTL in ways that facilitate positive changes based on new collaborative insights. As our examination of the TLA and our own experiences demonstrate, creating SoTL-PAR projects represents a powerful way to create positive changes in education and to provide transformative learning experiences not only for students but also for all of us.

Notes

1. We would like to thank James M. Hundley, Kathleen Saunders, and our "critical friends" Michael D. Sublett, Jeffrey A. Walsh, Kathleen McKinney, Denise Faigao, and Jessie L. Moore for their helpful comments on previous drafts of this chapter. We would also like to thank Alice McIntyre and Sage Publications for permission to reprint McIntyre's diagram.

References

Bradbury, H., & Reason, P. (2001). Broadening the bandwidth of validity: Issues and choice-points for improving the quality of action research. In P. Reason & H. Bradbury (Eds.), *Handbook of action research: Participative inquiry and practice* (pp. 447–455). London: Sage.

Ezzy, D. (2002). *Qualitative analysis: practice and innovation.* London: Routledge.

Fine, M., Torre, M. E., Boudin, K., Bowden, I., Clark, J., Hylton, D., Martinez, M., Rivera, M., Roberts, R. A., Smart, P., & Upegui, D. (2004). Participatory action research: From within and beyond prison bars. In L. Weis & M. Fine (Eds.), *Working method: Research and social justice* (pp. 95–119). New York: Routledge.

Fluehr-Lobban, C. (2008). Collaborative anthropology as twenty-first century ethical anthropology. *Collaborative Anthropologies, 1*(1), 175–182.

Freire, P. (2000). *Pedagogy of the oppressed* (M. B. Ramos, Trans). New York: Continuum. (Original work published 1970)

Greenwood, D. J., & Levin, M. (2007). *Introduction to action research: Social research for social change* (2nd ed.). Thousand Oaks, CA: Sage.

Kemmis, S., & McTaggart, R. (2005). Participatory action research: Communicative action and the public sphere. In N. K. Denzin & Y. S. Lincoln (Eds.), *The SAGE handbook of qualitative research* (3rd ed., pp. 559–604). Thousand Oaks, CA: Sage.

Lassiter, L. E. (2005). *The Chicago guide to collaborative ethnography.* Chicago: University of Chicago Press.

McIntyre, A. (2008). *Participatory action research.* Thousand Oaks, CA: Sage.

Neuman, W. L. (1997). *Social research methods: Qualitative and quantitative approaches* (3rd ed.). Boston: Allyn & Bacon.

Otis, M. M. (2010). *(En)powering students in the culture of higher education: The scholarship of teaching and learning as participatory action research.* Unpublished master's thesis, Western Washington University, Bellingham.

Ozer, E. J., Cantor, J. P., Cruz, G. W., Fox, B., Hubbard, E., & Moret, L. (2008). The diffusion of youth-led participatory research in urban schools: The role of the prevention support system in implementation and sustainability. *American Journal of Community Psychology, 41*(3/4), 278–289.

Reason, P. (1994). Human inquiry as discipline and practice. In P. Reason (Ed.), *Participation in human inquiry* (pp. 40–64). Thousand Oaks, CA: Sage.

Reason, P., & Bradbury, H. (2006). *Handbook of action research: The concise paperback edition.* Thousand Oaks, CA: Sage.

Schön, D. A. (1995). The new scholarship requires a new epistemology. *Change, 27*(6), 27–34.

Stewart, S., Riecken, T., Scott, T., Tanaka, M., & Riecken, J. (2008). Expanding health literacy: Indigenous youth creating videos. *Journal of Health Psychology, 13*(2), 180–189.

Stoecker, R. (2005). *Research methods for community change: A project-based approach.* Thousand Oaks, CA: Sage.

Stringer, E. T. (2007). *Action research* (3rd ed.). Los Angeles: Sage.

4

CHALLENGES AND CAVEATS

Betsy Newell Decyk, Michael Murphy,
Deborah G. Currier, and Deborah T. Long

This chapter is not about learning; it's about learning about learning *together.*[1] In the scholarship of teaching and learning (SoTL), we call this co-inquiry. While it can bring together faculty, student life professionals, administrators, and others, here we are focusing on what happens when we invite students into co-inquiry.

We do not intend to present a research report. It is neither data driven nor theory laden. It is existential and experiential. It results from sitting in classrooms and teaching with new practices. It comes from our observations, activities, and reflections. It comes from our experiences across our three institutions linked through the Carnegie Academy for the Scholarship of Teaching and Learning (CASTL) Institutional Leadership Program Student Voices theme group.

This chapter explores some of the challenges in the academic landscape and in ourselves that tend to constrain us from co-inquiry. These include issues of learning environments, role expectations, and developing the communication and trust that engender productive partnerships. The chapter provides some strategies and offers some warnings. However, co-inquiry as a practice is new and evolving. In each section we raise some questions that readers may have to answer from within their experiences and contexts.

The authors are dedicated to improving teaching and learning for all and to the belief that co-inquiry is a valuable way to proceed. As the author that has been involved with the CASTL student voices project from the beginning, I (Betsy Decyk) will narrate our collective story.

Challenge 1: External and Internalized Learning Spaces

Our student author, Michael Murphy, wrote:

> In my very first university class I realized my resistance to working with faculty carried over from high school to college. I had this almost indescribable fear of even approaching professors after class. Maybe it was all the knowledge the professors had or the university structure. I couldn't help but notice the hierarchical system that was laid out before me. I sat down in a class facing the backs of a hundred other students in a theater-like room. The wide expanse of the room narrowly pointing to the front, like an arrow pointing at the stage, showed me who was in power. That power, the hierarchical presence I found, kept me aware and reminded me every day who was in control, the person standing center stage. I couldn't even fathom the idea of speaking to my instructor. (M. Murphy, personal communication, October 27, 2008)

This description of a student's first college classroom experience reveals a nexus of challenges that impede learning by co-inquiry. The description makes us question, in particular, the educational space of the large lecture format, likely a typical experience for many students in their first 2 years at a university, and for some throughout their undergraduate years. As Michael so vividly described, the theaterlike setting concentrates attention to the stage and symbolically and literally transfers power to the professor. Furthermore, by layering rows of students, the physical space of the large lecture hall makes the professor nearly unapproachable. Finally, the seating of the students as the audience in a theater tends to reinforce their largely passive role in that setting.

The large lecture format, however, is merely an exaggerated example that reveals the relationship of physical space and behavioral expectations. Once we have become aware of the implicit influence of a space on learning, we can also reassess the typical 45-seat classroom. Although on a smaller scale, it still exerts some of the same influences of its theaterlike counterpart. The seating arrangement directs students' attention to the front of the classroom and to the professor; it places students and professor in opposition to one another, and students continue to occupy the role of audience.

In contrast, co-inquiry, as its own form of learning, requires at once a more egalitarian and a more active learning environment. In co-inquiry, students with faculty, student-life professionals, administrators, and possibly others share a common curiosity to learn about learning. Everyone becomes a learner and everyone becomes a teacher. Michael described his experience with co-inquiry in the Teaching-Learning Academy (TLA) at Western Washington University: "We talk about what is important to us and what we value as incoming students, new faculty members, senior administrators, transfer students, graduating seniors, and community members. We learn from each other and share our experiences while trying to improve our university" (for more on the TLA, see chapters 2 and 3). Co-inquiry spaces need to "invite all members of the learning community to engage in dialogue" (M. Murphy, personal communication, October 27, 2008).

To some extent, we can reconfigure existing traditional spaces for co-inquiry. In the traditional rectangular classroom, for example, one approach is to "circle up" so that participants create a unified inquiry space that does away with rows, levels, and status. A variation on this arrangement, which is especially useful if the circle of participants is too big for the room, is to create a double ring of seats. Having the people in the inner circle turn their chairs around so that they can converse with the people facing them can dispel the perception that these concentric circles might suggest a new hierarchy in terms of an inner circle. Having people move along the ring, switching circles as they switch seats to the left or to the right, also brings new people in conversation with each other.

Using spaces on campus that are not part of the regular classroom experience may be even more conducive to co-inquiry. One of the campus buildings may be a house with a living room, a dining room, or a patio that can be used for meetings. Some campuses can schedule campus events in conference centers. Meeting in a space of shared importance to the campus community, such as the library, provides a literal and metaphorical common ground. The change in the physical space from the classroom to one of these other types of venues signals to people that something different is happening. They are more conducive to new decor, including flowers, plants, and art, which can set a new tone for working together. Sometimes the mere change of locale is enough to disrupt the learned norms of communicating within the classroom setting. Encouraging the students to help search out a "found space" for meeting can serve the goal of collaboration itself and by its very nature not allow the normal communication hierarchies to take over.

The traditional architecture of educational settings holds us captive. The boxy classroom, with the teacher's desk at the front and rows of students' desks, and its larger counterpart, the amphitheater, serves primarily the lecture format of teaching and learning, reinforces the divide between the teacher and student, and encourages student passivity. For many faculty and their students, such spaces are so assumed that they, in contrast to students like Michael, don't even notice the constraints the space puts on them. Co-inquiry, however, calls for reconfiguring the spaces, and arrangements within spaces to foster active partnerships.

Caveats

Our notion of a physical space is more ingrained and internalized than we usually realize. Changing the physical space but failing to adjust our mental maps may undermine our good intentions. For instance, teachers may ask their students to circle up in the classroom but then place themselves in the circle in the area of the teacher's desk, the head of the classroom. Or they may continue to stand while the students are seated. The leaders of a group may use a conference room with a rectangular table but then place themselves at the head of the table. Co-inquiry, especially when it is starting, will probably have one or more leaders or facilitators. Thinking about how they place themselves is essential to making the paradigm shift necessary for group collaboration and co-inquiry.

Questions

What we have considered so far is the actual physical space of teaching and learning. Parker Palmer (1998), however, suggests a broader notion of space: "By space I mean a complex of factors: the physical arrangement and feeling in the room, the conceptual framework that I build around the topic my students and I are exploring, the emotional ethos I hope to facilitate, and the ground rules that will guide our inquiry" (p. 73). The dynamics of teaching and learning he encourages relies on "spatial" tensions or paradoxes. For example, the space should be hospitable (safe) and charged (filled with significant, challenging ideas). The space should welcome silence and speech. (See Appendix A for more about these paradoxes of space.) Palmer's work challenges us to consider learning spaces in more than just a physical way. What qualities should this broader space have to energize and sustain SoTL co-inquiry?

Challenge 2: Traditional Role Expectations

While Michael's description of his first college classroom experiences was primarily about the large lecture hall as a learning space, he also noted something else that may have contributed to his fear: "Maybe it was all the knowledge the professors had." In contrast, in describing his co-inquiry experiences, Michael wrote, "We sit in circles so everyone can face each other and wear name badges with just our first and last names, no titles" (M. Murphy, personal communication, October 27, 2008). In noting that they didn't use titles, he suggests that the expertise was not concentrated solely in the faculty but diffused throughout the circle.

All people have internalized expectations about how they should act (or not act) in certain situations and how they expect others to act (or not act) in those same situations. These largely implicit expectations influence all interpersonal interactions. Some of these expectations stem from roles that people play, and these role expectations determine to some extent the power relationships and other dynamics.

In co-inquiry, the members of the campus community can all be part of a collaborative partnership to learn about learning. Sharing the inquiry space in this way takes people out of their customary roles. Creating not just the physical space but also establishing a social environment where people can put aside familiar roles and expectations and assume new ones represents another challenge for SoTL co-inquiry.

Having name tags with names but not titles is one way to begin creating a new environment. Asking people to introduce themselves with their motives for participating rather than by their titles is also a good idea because it places them in partnership rather than in hierarchy. Icebreakers that reveal common interests also helps people to see each other as individuals and potential colleagues and to demystify the role of the professor.

Another way to decenter the usual role expectations is to distribute leadership across the group. People automatically assume the person calling the meeting is the leader of the project, and this assumption may be true for the duration of the project or for at least some time. However, the project leader should find ways to share power to ensure that each member of the group has a significant contributing role. For example, the convener might invite others to facilitate a session and step back into the group. This in turn changes the locus of power and the group dynamics in a way that makes co-inquiry possible. Sharing additional significant roles is another way to share power and strengthen the idea of partnership through mutual responsibility.

Caveats

Taking people out of their regular roles takes them away from the comfort zone of their usual expectations. Participants may register this difference as unsettling without articulating it, and reactions to it may surface in a variety of ways. People may feel fearful, uncertain, frustrated, challenged, or angry. Being able to articulate what is troubling to someone and being able to help others articulate what is troubling them leads more quickly to a possible solution than ignoring the problem.

Many of our role expectations are implicit and have likely gone unexamined. Some of our beliefs may be true and even well founded, but as Marchese (1997) points out, "Prior beliefs can be a major impediment to subsequent learning: beliefs may be objectively wrong, or bigoted, or dysfunctional, and block fair and open encounter with the new and the different" (p. 92). College professors who have assumed a very traditional top-down approach to teaching and learning, an approach they experienced in their own education, may be resistant to changing their beliefs or reimagining the student/professor relationship.

The same can be true for students as well. Another one of our authors, Deborah Long, shares the following cautionary story. While the story is about implementing problem-based learning in a class, the story is relevant to co-inquiry in SoTL projects as well.

> In one of my education classes I decided to use problem-based learning (PBL). The promise of PBL was appealing to me as an educator as I wanted my education students to become curious, thoughtful, motivated future teachers who could work collaboratively to solve serious problems in our public school system. I knew that PBL had a record of success in sparking curiosity and motivation in middle school students and thought that it was well worth considering as a tool to engage my college students as well (Kain, 2003). Given recent concerns regarding the growing teacher shortage, I designed a PBL unit entitled Teacher Quest to immerse my students in the issues surrounding teacher recruitment and retention. We were not too far along in the semester when I realized that the students in the class

were disgruntled, confused, and anxious. I had never before had an experience like this. I had always had an excellent rapport with my students and my teaching evaluations had always been quite good. Complaints in the class ranged from concerns about how I would grade student work to how I would differentiate between those who had worked hard and those who simply did the minimum—not unusual concerns.

It wasn't until I read my final evaluations, however, that the real issue came to light. Students wrote "We did all the work. You didn't do anything." Aha! So that was the problem. The teacher's role and the student's role are so deeply entrenched by the time a student comes to college that when the traditional (comfortable) roles are redefined, students may become upset. So often I hear my students remark, "Don't come to observe me today; I am not really teaching." When I ask what they will be doing, they reply, "Well, I have my students working in small groups on a project." The assumption is, of course, that if we are not giving students information, we are not teaching—we are not "doing the work of teaching." (D. T. Long, personal communication, October 21, 2008)

Established beliefs are very difficult to change. Another caveat, then, is that there is likely to be resistance to co-inquiry not only from people outside the group but also from members of the group. Deborah suggested that the recommendations for teacher education programs struggling with *belief persistence* (Yost, Sentner, & Forlenza-Bailey, 2000) may be applicable to SoTL co-inquiry. Creating opportunities and activities for people to reflect on their beliefs may be the cognitive catalyst for changing them (D. T. Long, personal communication, December 15, 2008). Deborah drew two other lessons from her PBL experience that can benefit those of us doing SoTL co-inquiry projects. The first was a lesson about preparation, "What I learned from this experience was how critically important it is that we prepare not only ourselves, but also our students for the shift in power and responsibility when we alter the dynamics in the classroom." The second was a lesson about the outcome, "We should not deceive ourselves that giving/sharing power with the students will be welcomed by all of them" (D. T. Long, personal communication, October 21, 2008).

Finally, while in co-inquiry we have new roles and develop new expectations, we are never that far from our regular roles and the usual expectations that can intrude at any time. To complicate matters, some intrusion of the traditional roles and expectations may be necessary. For example, when an

SoTL co-inquiry accompanies a class or an independent study project for credit, the teacher(s) involved will have to evaluate and certify the student's work. Faculty who supervise students may also be partners with them in co-inquiry projects. These dual roles of partner-student, partner-teacher, partner-supervisor may create ethical dilemmas, conflicts of interest, and strains in interpersonal relationships. Clarity about the existence of these dualities, the honest recognition of their potential implications, and care in managing them become extremely important.

Questions

It is customary now to think of co-inquiry in terms of sharing: decision making and power, work and responsibility, research findings, and opportunities to present them. Research on learning, however, demonstrates that an expert organizes knowledge around core concepts in his or her field, whereas novices "are more likely to approach problems by searching for correct formulas and pat answers that fit their everyday intuitions" (Bransford, Brown, & Cocking, 2000, p. 49). Is it always appropriate to share decision making and other responsibilities? In some cases might there be a different role for those in the group who have the most expertise? Is there ever a time when traditional roles are more productive for all involved? Are there situations in which co-inquiry may impede progress or may not be feasible because of time constraints? As a SoTL co-inquiry group begins, and as it evolves, it will probably have to grapple with these and related questions.

Challenge 3: Bringing Co-Inquiry to Life

New expectations and interactions will evolve from the initially unfamiliar roles of a co-inquiry partnership. Students and educators alike may harbor anxiety and even fear about changing the dynamics. It is important to remind everyone involved in co-inquiry that they are embarking on the unfamiliar, and that traditional roles and relationships will shift or be transformed altogether. How do we prepare the participants for these changes? How do we instill the trust that participants need to have in themselves and others to fully engage in the collaboration? How do we provide safety so that participants will contribute creatively? How do we nurture the new dynamic?

One way to establish trust may be to apply the Creating, Performing, and Responding (CPR) method of learning. CPR, which is the arts motto of the Washington State Office of Superintendent of Public Instruction, can be applied to any area of teaching and learning as a method of organizing and approaching the work (see http://www.k12.wa.us/curriculuminstruct/arts). One of our authors, Deb Currier, a theater professor, explained the benefits of CPR this way:

> CPR is a method of breathing life into collaborative scholarship. Art educators use it when collaborative inquiry is embedded in daily activities, rehearsals, and performances. It allows for all collaborators to invest, share, and reap the rewards of safe and productive inquiry. (D. G. Currier, personal communication, October 20, 2008)

According to Deb, the components of SoTL co-inquiry that correspond to CPR in the arts are creating or defining questions, beliefs, goals, and aspirations; performing or active co-research, mentoring, and leadership; and responding or co-presenting and sharing the findings. SoTL and CPR both involve learning in action, collaboration, and creativity.

While CPR may provide a theoretical framework for co-inquiry participants, its real value is in the exercises and activities that give the participants an experiential basis for working together. Because the foundation of CPR is based in arts education, many of the exercises and activities are derived from traditional performing arts warm-ups, icebreakers, and exercises. An example of just one activity involves inviting a group to create a *collaborative machine*.[2] The machine begins with one person creating a nonverbal moving part of what will become a complex machine involving everyone in the group. Each participant adds on, one at a time, interacting nonverbally in a repetitive, physical way. The key element of this exercise is that each person becoming a part of the machine must add on in a way that makes him or her part of the whole machine, not a separate cog disassociated from what is being built together. Participants add their own repetitive motion to build the machine until the whole group eventually is one large, whirring, buzzing, moving (and usually laughing) physical embodiment of collaboration. When we did this as an icebreaker for a new SoTL co-inquiry group, there was some hesitation at first, but eventually everyone was part of our animated machine in one way or another. This exercise moved us rapidly out of our regular roles while showing us that with our combined ingenuities, we could create something together without using words. We each had to do our part while trusting that others would do theirs so the machine wouldn't break down. And the good humor of it all broke up our new-to-the-group shyness.

Nonverbal exercises and activities such as the collaborative machine ask us to experience, move, and interact without our usual verbal overlay.

> In an environment that has traditionally shut down or silenced the creative voice of many students and faculty alike, it can be extremely beneficial to take time and energy to establish an imaginative, resourceful and innovative atmosphere from the beginning. For many of us, verbal communication is power—the person who speaks eloquently, the most, or even sometimes just the loudest can immediately shift and realign authority structures in a group, thereby inhibiting the concept of sharing power. In the traditional verbal learning set-up, learners pick up very quickly on the power structure enabled by verbal communication. So, what if we take that away? What if we, as a group, explored, posed, examined a topic or a question non-verbally first, then used our realizations and discoveries through the exercise to begin discussion on a verbal level, starting with what we have seen or felt in creating our response? (D. G. Currier, personal communication, October 20, 2008)

As a learning tool for SoTL co-inquiry groups, nonverbal activities may be an initial way to reset the group dynamic and provide each person with a new starting point for interactions.

While it is one challenge to move away from our reliance on words, it's another challenge to develop ways of using words that serve the new dynamic of co-inquiry. We offer a few examples here, which are described in the endnotes for this chapter.

- The "This I believe" assignment (inspired by essays featured on National Public Radio and collected at http://www.thisibelieve.org) can help each member of the group uncover a deeply held personal value and discover an authentic voice (see Appendix B).
- Dichotic listening (psychology) generally convinces people that we don't often listen well and could do better.[3]
- Active listening (conflict resolution studies) can provide practice in attending to the speaker (and not to one's own response to the speaker).[4]

- Conversational analysis (linguistics) helps people become aware of the variety of conversational styles people have even within the same language and understand how conflicts can flare surprisingly quickly from mismatches in these styles.[5]
- Role playing with shifting roles expands participants' understanding of a problem, issue, or position.[6]
- Brainstorming (conflict resolution studies), which truly separates the generation of ideas from any judgment or evaluation, provides practice for the open-minded discussion of options before decision making.[7]
- The "Telling Selves" assignment (Appendix C) blends nonverbal, verbal, visual, kinesthetic, and emotional elements to facilitate a group dynamic of collaboration through sharing and actually performing the words, actions, and deepest-held beliefs of group members.

Caveats

Trust, especially new trust, is fragile. The excitement and energy that initially goes into a SoTL co-inquiry group can wane when people assume new responsibilities or commitments. Old habits of power and passivity die hard. Faculty may change positions or retire. Students graduate. Sustaining co-inquiry as a viable research approach in SoTL takes vigilance and effort.

Questions

In this section we share activities from our respective fields of experience that empower people to engage in the new dynamic of co-inquiry. However, each co-inquiry group will have its own representation of academic disciplines as well as differing background experiences of its participants. What additional resources and activities will create open communication and build trust?

Conclusion

As we learned from the first iteration of the CASTL Student Voices cluster group (2003–2006), the principles for sustaining student voices in co-inquiry need to be ecological: "Rather than imagining education as a river which flows from the teacher to the student, it would be better to think of education as a whole ecosystem which is both dynamic and interactive" (for this

set of eco-principles, see http://www.wwu.edu/studentvoices/svccp.shtml).
These how-to principles suggest, in part, an action plan for including students in SoTL research and preserving their legacy.

After 3 more years of co-inquiry with students, we realize further that
partners in co-inquiry must see themselves not just as members and participants in a very special educational ecosystem, and not just the developers of
knowledge in SoTL, but also as the stewards of the new human relationships
essential to co-inquiry success. This is the true basis of co-inquiry's sustainability as a methodological approach.

Notes

1. We sincerely thank the Carnegie Academy Institutional Leadership Program
(CASTL) 2006–2009, which made the co-authorship of this chapter possible. We
are deeply grateful to Carmen Werder of Western Washington University for her
leadership of the CASTL Student Voices group, and to Megan Otis, also of Western
Washington University, for their editorial perseverance and perspicuity. In addition,
we thank our critical friends, Kathleen McKinney, Patricia Jarvis, Gary Creasey,
Derek Herrmann, Ellen Gutman, Erin M. Sergison, Chelsea J. Martin, and Jeffrey
L. Bernstein for their encouragement and formative comments on our amorphous
first draft.

2. The collaborative machine is an exercise found in almost every basic acting
and improvisation textbook. For more exercises and activities of this nature, see
Spolin (1986) and Novelly (1985).

3. The dichotic listening exercise involves three people, A, B, and C. C sits in
the center, and A and B sit on either side. A reads from one text at the same time
that B reads from a different text. C is told to attend to what A is reading. When A
and B are finished reading, C is asked about what B read (instead of what A read).
Usually C cannot recall much of the text from B's reading because C was paying
attention to A's text. Extending this to our own conversations, when we listen to
someone speaking, we often are not really listening carefully to that person but listening to ourselves formulating our response to what the person is saying.

4. Practice concentrating on a speaker's verbal message and the accompanying
nonverbal behavior. Active listening often involves mirroring, paraphrasing, or
reframing what the person said and asking for correction and clarification.

5. Conversational analysis involves listening to and analyzing short conversation
samples, especially ones where people end up in conflict. The paradigm case is Deborah Tannen's (1990) example of the husband and wife who are driving somewhere
together. The wife asks the husband if he would like to stop for a cup of coffee. The
husband says no. The wife then gets angry. The typical analysis of what happened
in this short conversation is that the wife was using indirect speech (she wanted a

cup of coffee but did not say that directly). The husband, however, reflected and decided he was not thirsty and answered no (missing the indirect hint that the wife wanted to stop for coffee).

6. Role plays with shifting roles involves making up a scenario with several characters (for example, a mother, a grandfather, a teenager, and a neighbor, each with a particular perspective). The scenario may seem simple at first but becomes more complex as it continues. During breaks in the scenario people have to switch roles and take a different perspective on the scenario.

7. The rule of thumb for brainstorming is that all options, including outrageous or humorous ones, should be generated without evaluative comments to make sure the brainstorming is not truncated too early by negative remarks. In practice this is very hard to do. The exercise is to brainstorm a solution to some problem without evaluation.

References

Bransford, J., Brown, A., & Cocking, R. (Eds.). (2000). *How people learn: Brain, mind, experience, and school.* Washington, DC: National Academy Press.

Kain, D. L. (2003). *Problem-based learning for teachers, grades K–8.* Boston: Allyn & Bacon.

Marchese, T. (1997). The new conversations about learning: Insights from neuroscience and anthropology, cognitive science and work-place studies. In E. E. Chaffee (Ed.), *Assessing impact: Evidence and action* (pp. 79–95). Washington, DC: American Association for Higher Education.

Novelly, M. C. (1985). *Theatre games for young performers: Improvisations and exercises for developing acting skills.* Colorado Springs, CO: Meriwether.

Palmer, P. (1998). *The courage to teach.* San Francisco, CA: Jossey-Bass.

Spolin, Viola. (1986). *Theatre games for the classroom: A teacher's handbook.* Evanston, IL: Northwestern University Press.

Tannen, D. (1990). *You just don't understand: Women and men in conversation.* New York: William Morrow.

Yost, D., Sentner, S., & Forlenza-Bailey, A. (2000). An examination of the construct of critical reflection: Implications for teacher education programming in the 21st century. *Journal of Teacher Education, 51*(1), 39–50.

Appendix A

Parker Palmer's (1998) Paradoxes

Paradox #1. The space should be bounded and open.

The space should use the text, data, and questions to focus thinking. The teacher and the materials provide the boundaries, however the space must be

open to many paths. "If boundaries remind us that our journey has a destination, openness reminds us that there are many ways to reach that end"
(p. 75).

Paradox #2. The space should be hospitable and "charged."

The space should be safe and open but also filled with significant, challenging ideas.

*Paradox #3. The space should invite the voice of the individual and the
voice of the group.*

The space should be more than a place for individual expression. It should
be a place where "the group can affirm, question, challenge, and correct the
voice of the individual" (p. 75).

*Paradox #4. The space should honor the "little" stories of the students
and the "big" stories of the disciplines and tradition.*

The student stories (ideas) and the stories (ideas) of the discipline must both
be told and respected so that greater insight can be gained.

*Paradox #5. The space should support solitude and surround it with
the resources of community.*

Learning requires time to reflect and absorb, but it also requires a community where ideas can be tested, challenged, and our understanding refined.

Paradox #6. The space should welcome both silence and speech.

We educate with silence as well as speech. Silence should not be interpreted
as something gone wrong.

Paradox #7. The space should encourage playfulness and responsibility.

Learning requires risk taking, stepping outside the box, and pushing the
boundaries. Playing with ideas and possibilities must be welcomed and yet
this playfulness must be balanced with the development of responsibility, an
understanding of the significance of the learning enterprise.

Appendix B

"This I Believe" Essay Assignment

This activity was the first assignment given to students in a Theatre for Social
Change course at Western Washington University. The idea was that before

the students could engage in the theories and methods of social change, they needed to identify and share their own core values. The students and professor simultaneously posted their essays on the Blackboard Web site at exactly 3:00 p.m. on the date due to ensure more honest responses. For details see the National Public Radio *This I Believe Discussion Manual at* http://www.npr.org/thisibelieve.

Sample Activity

TIB Icebreaker

Done in class when the assignment was explained—make sure students and professor participate together.

- Post signs in different corners/spaces in the room that read Strongly Agree, Agree, Disagree, and Strongly Disagree. (*Post signs before students arrive to generate immediate interest.*)
- Read out loud the following explanation and follow it with the exercise:

The following statements are just a few of the axioms people hold to be true in their life. As I read each statement, stand beneath the sign that is true for you. The first part of this exercise is nonverbal—try not to indicate or show judgment of others' beliefs as you move about the room!

What Do You Think?

- Life is fair.
- Words can hurt.
- What goes around comes around.
- How you act in a crisis shows who you really are.
- Love conquers all.
- An eye for an eye.
- People learn from their mistakes.
- You can't depend on anyone else; you can only depend on yourself.
- If you smile long enough you become happy.
- Miracles do happen.
- Money can't buy happiness.
- Killing is wrong.
- Doing what is right means obeying the law.

At the end of the kinesthetic activity, ask participants to share the statements they would *add* to the list.

Group discussion/thinking points (back in seats/circle): For those statements you agreed with, how did you come to that position? For those you did not agree with, why?

Appendix C

"Telling Selves" Assignment

Created by Professor Deb Currier for her Theatre for Social Change course at Western Washington University

Telling Selves Interview Assignment

Pair students and give guidelines for interviewing each other for the purpose of creating a performance piece.

Directions: Without too much personal editing—we're going for free-flowing thoughts!—ask your partner to list his or her

- Disapprovals
- Movie or pop culture moments he or she adores
- "Family truths"
- Losses
- Blessings
- Secret fetishes
- Physical injuries
- Envies
- Nicknames

Ask students to create a performance piece using the answers and information given by their partner.

Rules for Creating Your Performance

- You must work with your partner and accept all changes he or she wishes you to make.
- You may only use the words of your partner.
- You must include at least three props.

- You must have a costume of some kind.
- You have 5 minutes total, and *both parts should be equal.*
- You must both come up with a transition that weaves the two parts together.
- You must include music of some kind.

Ask partners to combine their performance pieces into one 5-minute performance presentation per pair for the class.

5

INVOKING THE *L* IN THE SCHOLARSHIP OF LEARNING AND TEACHING

Jane Verner and William Harrison Lay

The traditional model of a teacher-centered classroom in which the teacher is the primary decision maker and the sole deliverer of knowledge still tends to dominate. Because standing in front of a class and expecting participants to be interested and engaged raises a number of serious philosophical, ethical, and efficacy issues, when Western Washington University began its affiliation with the Carnegie Academy for the Scholarship of Teaching and Learning (CASTL) in 1999, our focus and distinguishing feature became listening to the student voices silenced in that model. Listening to those long-silenced student voices as well as to the voices of others invested in the scholarship of learning and teaching, the authors, two faculty in Western Washington University's Woodring College of Education, crafted a collaborative approach emphasizing full participatory engagement that is attentive to all voices, and the results can be used to inform and transform future practices. The nontraditional, learner-centered model presented in this chapter accentuates not only hearing all learner voices in a genuinely equal partnership of collaborative discourse but also engages all learners in a dynamic process through which unlearning/relearning, choice, and taking advantage of the unexpected occurs.

An initial problem faced in constructing this collaborative model of learning was developing a language that articulated another way of naming, describing, and analyzing the learning cycle. The language people use not

only reveals their reality but also limits it. Our ways of thinking about education are limited by semantics, and because the only language frequently
accessible to us is encapsulated by the traditional model, appropriate termi-
nology needs to be developed.

For example, the language of *student-teacher* inherently implies a power
hierarchy in which knowledge resides only with the teacher and in which the
students tend to be silenced; they are passive recipients of the concepts and
thoughts taught to them by the sage on the stage. Truly transformative education demands that learners be active participants in the process, not merely
recipients of information banked in their consciousness by a teacher talking
at them (Freire, 1970), however entertaining that teacher might be. In contrast, the language of *learning colleagues* implies something entirely different—an equal partnership in the learning environment! It is a more inclusive
language that evokes a way of viewing the interactional nature of those
engaged in learning. The term *learning colleagues* implies that all those
involved are mutually invested in successful learning; as a community they
co-create a safe, supportive, dynamic environment where each individual's
views and beliefs are heard, deeply valued, and generously supported. It
denotes a process that encourages learners to simultaneously examine how
they individually learn, as well as how groups learn collectively.

Learning colleagues reflects a process through which hearing the "plural-
ity of voices" (Fielding, 2004, p. 302) inherently expands and extends learning; it exposes participants to diverse backgrounds, perspectives, and thought
processes. The process reveals viewpoints from people in all walks of life and
in so doing addresses important issues of diversity. Equally important,
according to Zúñiga, Nagda, Chesler, & Cytron-Walker (2007), this type of
dialogue opens myriad paths for learning as participants delve into the subject matter while considering others' opinions. It promotes the realization
that through interaction with others, everyone teaches and learns; all participants become "co-directors and co-editors of their social world" (McWilliam, 2008, p. 267).

Although we believe the language used to explore, define, and describe
the learning process is extremely important, including learners as equal partners demands far more than merely adopting a language of possibility (Giroux, 1992). According to Poindexter (2006), effective educators also need to
authentically listen to "all stakeholders and incorporate what they hear into
their priorities" (p. 19). Even then, the erroneous assumption often persists

that what the teacher teaches, the students learn (Davis, Smith, & Leflore, 2008; Rodgers, 2006). Furthermore, as noted by Black (2005), using collaborative discourse as a methodology for learning is problematic with large classes unless learners are broken into small groups and/or unless we take advantage of alternative modes of dialogue that exist outside the traditional classroom, such as electronic discussion boards or blogs. Smaller groups and electronic dialogue intrinsically offer a greater opportunity to hear all voices and develop the feelings of trust and safety that truly educative discourse demands (Rodgers). According to Martindale (Martindale & Wiley, 2005), blogs also have "a greater sense of permanence" (p. 59) and can be used as a tool for learning long after a class ends.

Providing genuine choices for learners and using various methodological approaches to appeal to different learning styles (Davis et al., 2008; Garlick, 2008; Poindexter, 2006; Rodgers, 2006) must also be artfully applied, but even then relinquishing control remains challenging for some faculty. Becoming truly equal partners in learning often requires a personal paradigm shift on the part of those involved, which in turn requires not only a willingness to change but the courage to explore new approaches (Zúñiga et al., 2007).

Rodgers (2006) noted, "Giving students a voice in and power over their own learning can be a revelation" (p. 230). It is also revolutionary that classrooms are converted into democratic learning environments, interactive and learner centered, where co-inquiry becomes the norm. In the model presented in this chapter, teachers no longer are constrained in their role as actors on the classroom stage but become partners in the process of exploration and discovery. This method of discovery is itself a tool that further reveals what helps students learn and what constrains their learning. Cultivating reflection and strengthening enduring dispositions toward learning are inherent outcomes of this collaborative learning experience because the process itself exposes and identifies various strategies to further enhance the learner's voice.

Collaborative Learning Model Activity

Initially designed for use with groups of 20 to 30 participants, this approach is fitting for classrooms and professional development workshops with varied participants: students, faculty, staff, and administrators. Though originally intended to be about 2 to 4 hours in duration, it can be readily adapted for shorter or longer time frames.

Four interconnected focus areas—unlearning/relearning, partnership, choice, and the unanticipated—are central to developing empowered engagement and serve as the focus topics to be investigated in this collaborative activity. The description and details provided below allow for modifications depending on outcomes and needs of the participants and facilitators. Considerable latitude in design is possible; the activity can easily be tailor made by varying the types of materials and music used.

Room Preparation

Prior to conducting this learning experience, facilitators secure a room with adequate space to comfortably accommodate the total number of participants, and equip the area with tables and chairs that easily can be rearranged. The process begins and ends with participants grouped in plenary yet for the most part uses small discussion tables of between five and eight people, so the room size and the furniture available are important factors to consider. Music establishes a welcoming environment and provides a transition between separate segments of the activity, so include a portable sound system for flexibility. Facilitators choose a total of seven appropriate musical selections—one for entering the room, another for ending the initial plenary session, three for moving between the focus tables, one for returning to plenary, and a final selection or medley for closing the activity.

Properly setting up the room is important. Four tables and enough chairs for everyone need to be available. Prior to the start of the activity, arrange the chairs in a circle in the center of the room, with a table located in each corner of the room. As the activity proceeds from plenary to small group, participants move their chairs to the initial tables where they work and later return them to the plenary circle for summative discussion and closure.

Materials

Provide a blank flip chart page or secure a large section of butcher paper on the wall beside each corner table. Prior to the final debriefing, collect these sheets and move them to a centrally located spot in the room; set each table as if for a dinner party with sheets of colored construction paper serving as place mats and colored markers as utensils. Assign each table a separate color, and place a small stock of extra color-coded construction paper in the center of each table for use if needed. In addition to the place mat sheets and marker utensils, position a color-coordinated instruction booklet specific to each table (described in the following section, "The Process.") on the center of each place mat as if it were a menu. Provide enough extra menus in the middle of the table so all the participants (20–30) have one as they make the rounds from table to table as the activity progresses.

The Process

The dialogue begins with participants seated in a plenary circle with the facilitator engaging everyone in brief introductions. This conversation is vitally important, for creating a community of learners early in the process will pay significant dividends as the dialogue proceeds. If individuals are not familiar with each other, brief biographical information can be shared; whereas if they already belong to a learning community, time can be spent primarily on describing the upcoming activity. After giving directions and explanations of the process, facilitators ask participants to retain the information as a reference for the rest of the activity.

After building the requisite sense of community among the participants, individuals self-select a focus table of special interest, and prompted by an appropriate musical score, take their chairs and sit at their chosen table. It is also prudent to have extra writing instruments and construction paper available at each table for individuals to use for note taking during the dialogue. At each table a volunteer assumes the role of recorder/reporter and everyone reads the table's instruction booklet, or menu, that provides the table's specific focus topic, a corresponding quote, and a series of prompts intended to initiate conversation. Dialogue related to the provided topic ensues. Each table's reporter uses the color-coordinated marker and construction or butcher paper to record and post group members' ideas on the focus topic. The discussion continues until the facilitators indicate with an appropriate musical score that it is time for the groups to progress to a new focus topic by moving clockwise to the next table. While recorders remain at their initial table posting their notes from the previous dialogue on the butcher paper or flip chart sheet, the other participants rotate to the next table.

As participants sit at their new tables, the recorder/reporter briefs them on previous insights about that particular table's focus topic and then engages them in their own dialogue to further explore and expand upon the topic. Participants repeat the process (with the exception of the recorders who, for continuity purposes, remain at their initial tables) until they travel to all four tables and discuss each of the focus topics. Once individuals engage in dialogue at each table, music signals the end of the process and participants take their chairs and rejoin the larger circle in preparation for the summative dialogue.

During the summative dialogue, table reporters use their posted records to review the topic explorations and resulting insights from their respective tables. The participants discuss in plenary the interrelationships among and between the topic areas and the richness of perceptions drawn forth during the collaboration. A final selection of music prompts facilitators to bring closure to the session by distributing an evaluation form and asking participants to complete and return it prior to leaving the room. After reflecting upon the experience and reviewing the recorders' records as well as the evaluation forms, facilitators condense the findings from each table into a final commentary that can later be made available to participants.

Investigating the Four Interconnected Focus Areas

Unlearning/relearning, partnership, choice, and the unanticipated are believed by the authors to be crucial to effective collaborative learning. It is these four interconnected focus areas that participants explore during the collaborative activity.

1. Focus Area—Unlearning/Relearning

This focus topic develops and reinforces the understanding that learning inherently implies change, and that what we believe or think we know deserves thorough reflection, analysis, and perhaps even reconstruction. Wink (2005) referred to this process of unlearning and relearning as "the great cycle of pedagogy" (p. 67). Some assumptions that have emerged about unlearning/relearning include

- Learners will not attend class unless there is an incentive to attend.
- Passing the class is the most important aspect of the learning cycle.
- There is only one right answer to any given question, and only one right way to get to that answer.
- Learners begin class with no knowledge and teachers are the experts.
- Professors are not teaching if they are not lecturing.

- It is neither safe to learn by mistakes nor acceptable to make them.
- Students cannot learn from each other and have nothing to contribute to the conversation.

Transformation   The intended transformative outcomes of exploring this focus topic are (a) to create an awareness among the learning colleagues that the traditional model of knowledge transmission is often based upon preconceived assumptions that preclude deep and lasting learning, and (b) to elicit the realization that a more inclusive model that promotes self-reliance and cultivates enduring dispositions toward learning may not only be possible but preferable.

Process at This Table   Participants in this topic grouping identify and record preconceptions and assumptions about the teaching/learning cycle that might need to be unlearned and suggest new ways of thinking and behaving to replace them.

Example   A common example of one such preconception is that learners will not attend class unless attendance is taken. This assumption may be based upon the belief that learning is dull, boring, and undesirable, that learning must for some reason be coerced. Perhaps this supposition needs to be unlearned and replaced with the acknowledgment that motivation for learning is intrinsic to human nature and is a primary characteristic of the human condition. Lessons with personal significance will naturally engage the learners!

Sample Quotation to Prompt Dialogue   "Our old views constrain us. They deprive us from engaging fully with this universe of potentialities" (Wheatley, 1992, p. 73).

2. Focus Area—Partnership

This focus topic develops and reinforces the understanding that equalizing power and control dynamics in the classroom requires thinking about students and faculty as learning colleagues, equal partners in the learning community (Rodgers, 2006; see also Davis et al., 2008; Freire, 1970; hooks, 2003; McWilliam, 2008; Zaiss, 2002).

Transformation   The intended transformative outcome of this focus topic is developing among participants the disposition to shift from the traditional model of a teacher-centered classroom to a more egalitarian model that equalizes the power and control dynamics of classroom interaction, embraces more fully all voices, and converts classrooms into more democratic learning environments.

Process at This Table   Participants in this focus topic's discussion identify and record strategies and practices that might equalize the power and control dynamics of classroom interaction.

Example   Fielding (2004) discussed some of the problems with the "largely anachronistic structures and cultures that still condition our practices" (p. 309). One strategy that could encourage a more egalitarian learning culture might be altering the language we use to refer to the participants. Instead of using dichotomous terms like *teacher* and *student* that inherently transmit messages about differences in power and control, terms like *classroom partners* or *learning colleagues* could be used.

Sample Quotation to Prompt Dialogue   "Competition rooted in dehumanizing practices of shaming, of sado-masochistic rituals of power, preclude communalism and stand in the way of community" (hooks, 2003, p. 131).

3. Focus Area–Choice

Discussing this focus topic develops and reinforces the understanding that truly meaningful learning occurs only when it is personally significant and self-directed. Learners can more easily own their education when it involves genuine options in terms of forming groups, selecting reading materials, and establishing research agendas.

Transformation   The transformative outcome of this focus topic is the disposition among participants to develop a deeper level of learner engagement by acknowledging differentiated learning styles and modes of expression, and by allowing all participants choices in the learning process that are truly meaningful and self-determined.

Process at This Table   Participants in the dialogue on this focus topic identify and record strategies that enable individuals to tailor learning opportunities that take into consideration their uniquely diverse lived experiences that best match their preferred mode of expression.

Example   McWilliam (2005) cautioned about the resistance learners might have when working in teams if their work is being assessed. To overcome this resistance, faculty can use creative methods of assessment such as co-designing a rubric with learners. Individual learners might have the opportunity to choose their own mode (such as writing an essay, producing a video, or creating a Web page) of demonstrating the degree and depth of learning that has occurred. The instructor can facilitate this opportunity by being flexible in assessment strategies and by ensuring that all assessment is individualized and differentiated.

Sample Quotation to Prompt Dialogue   "The function of the child is to live his own life—not the life that his anxious parents think he should live, nor a life according to the purpose of the educator who thinks he knows best" (A. S. Neill's Summerhill, 2004).

4. Focus Area—The Unanticipated

This topic area develops and reinforces the realization that effective lesson plans should be thought of as adaptive and evolutionary; they are not immutable ends unto themselves but rather synergistic and an ever-evolving means to a much greater end. At their very best, lesson plans are guides to a process, not paths to a specific end product.

Transformation   The transformative objective of this topic is the disposition among participants to move from a teaching/learning model that is rigidly standardized in its curriculum and instructional strategy to one that provides opportunities to explore strands of inquiry that are inevitably evoked by discourse and unexpectedly emerge during collective learning efforts (Davis et al., 2008).

Process at This Table   Participants in this focus topic's dialogue identify and record strategies for the classroom to become a dynamic laboratory to explore the interdisciplinary totality of the human experience rather than study fragmented and isolated bits of knowledge.

Example   One strategy that facilitates taking advantage of the unexpected is adding a blog or online discussion forum to the more traditional face-to-face mode of dialogue. Using an electronic medium provides the requisite time and flexibility to encourage learners to investigate uniquely individual insights that inevitably occur during protracted discussion. Another effective strategy might be to actually leave the confines of the classroom and transport the lesson to other appropriate venues on campus or in the community. At Western Washington University, options include viewing an art show at the Western Gallery of the College of Fine and Performing Arts; listening to a distinguished speaker invited to campus; participating in an event at Woodring College of Education's Center for Education, Equity, and Diversity; attending a play produced, directed, designed, and performed by learning colleagues from the theatre arts department; and meeting with representatives from local community agencies at their organization's location.

Sample Quotation to Prompt Dialogue   "In the teacher-directed lesson, the discussion was locked into a single, inflexible point with no possibility of movement" (Davis et al., 2008, p. 46).

A Collaborative Invitation

The general procedures and processes of the collaborative model of learning described in this chapter evolved over the years as the authors began to truly *hear* their learning colleagues' voices. Some faculty consider learner-centered approaches problematic because they emphasize outcome-based learning that has resulted from the accountability and assessment movement. Our response to those arguments is that standardization, accountability, and assessment need not always be viewed as obstacles; they can be seen as opportunities to advance and reinforce the importance of learners' voices. Indeed, accountability and requirements to meet standards do present significant tension when endeavoring to equalize power and control dynamics in class and to create equal partnerships with learners, but this tension can itself be the focus of analysis and critical thought. Discussions on how learners can more effectively gain knowledge within the parameters of such mandated factors can be very productive not only in terms of better understanding the tensions they create but in terms of how to use those tensions to enhance the learning experience. Dialogue on what it means to take responsibility for learning often leads to a better understanding of how we can collaboratively meet that responsibility.

It is also helpful when addressing resistance toward developing a more egalitarian learning culture that truly listens to the voices of all involved in the process to remember Rilke's (1934/2004) observation that if one embraces the questions, answers will emerge in their own time. The written words of chapters such as this one do not provide much opportunity for collaboration between the authors and you, the readers. As a remedy to that, and in the spirit of co-inquiry, we invite you to join us in listening to learners' voices, to invoke the *L* (the learning) in the process, and to share your ideas and insights by contacting us and bringing the collaborative process advocated in this chapter full circle. Together we can emphasize the learning, as implied in our title, and further advance the "scholarship of teaching and learning."

References

A. S. Neill's Summerhill. (2004). Retrieved from http://www.summerhillschool .co.uk/pages/asneill.html

Black, L. (2005). Dialogue in the lecture hall: Teacher-student communication and students' perceptions of their learning. *Qualitative Research Reports in Communication, 6*(1), 31–40.

Davis, E. J., Smith, T. J., & Leflore, D. (2008). *Chaos in the classroom: A new theory of teaching and learning.* Durham, NC: Carolina Academic Press.

Fielding, M. (2004). Transformative approaches to student voice: Theoretical underpinnings, recalcitrant realities. *British Educational Research Journal, 30*(2), 295–311.

Freire, P. (1970). *Pedagogy of the oppressed* (M. B. Ramos, Trans.) New York: Continuum.

Garlick, S. (2008). Can we hear the student voice? *Management in Education, 22*(3), 15–18.

Giroux, H. A. (1992). *Border crossings: Cultural workers and the politics of education.* New York: Routledge.

hooks, b. (2003). *Teaching community: A pedagogy of hope.* New York: Routledge.

Martindale, T., & Wiley, D. A. (2005). Using weblogs in scholarship and teaching. *TechTrends: Linking Research & Practice to Improve Learning, 49*(2), 55–61.

McWilliam, E. (2005). Unlearning pedagogy. *Journal of Learning Design, 1*(1), 1–11.

McWilliam, E. (2008). Unlearning how to teach. *Innovations in Education & Teaching International, 45*(3), 263–269.

Poindexter, M. C. (2006). Are colleges listening to students? *Connection, New England's Journal of Higher Education, 20*(4), 19–20.

Rilke, R. M. (2004). *Letters to a young poet* (M. D. Herter Norton, Trans.). New York: Norton. (Original work published 1934)

Rodgers, C. R. (2006). Attending to student voice: The impact of descriptive feedback on learning and teaching. *Curriculum Inquiry, 36*(2), 209–237.

Wheatley, M. J. (1992). *Leadership and the new science: Learning about organization from an orderly universe.* San Francisco: Berrett-Koehler.

Wink, J. (2005). *Critical pedagogy: Notes from the real world* (3rd ed.). Boston: Allyn & Bacon.

Zaiss, C. (2002). *True partnership: Revolutionary thinking about relating to others.* San Francisco: Berrett-Koehler.

Zúñiga, X., Nagda, B. A., Chesler, M., & Cytron-Walker, A. (2007). *Intergroup dialogue in higher education: Meaningful learning about social justice.* San Francisco: Jossey-Bass.

PART TWO

ENACTMENT

6

A RANGE OF STUDENT VOICES IN THE SCHOLARSHIP OF TEACHING AND LEARNING

Kathleen McKinney, Patricia Jarvis,
Gary Creasey, and Derek Herrmann

O ur chapter discusses a range of ways that student voices can be an integral part of the scholarship of teaching and learning (SoTL).[1] We focus on student voices in SoTL where SoTL is defined as the "systematic reflection on teaching and learning made public" (Illinois State University, 2009). Thus, we emphasize student voices in SoTL research projects, but we define research broadly because of disciplinary differences. Furthermore, recognizing that other institutions may define SoTL more broadly than this, we include brief discussions of student voices in scholarly teaching and teaching improvement.

Earlier chapters include discussions of the theoretical underpinnings of involving students in SoTL. Thus, we begin with a sample of the empirical literature on the value of student involvement and voices in research generally that relates to SoTL research specifically. Next we present a continuum or range of possible roles that students can play in SoTL followed by some concrete examples of students in these various roles at three institutions in the Carnegie Academy for the Scholarship of Teaching and Learning (CASTL) Institutional Leadership Program Student Voices theme group. We emphasize the value of these roles for our community of learners generally and for the SoTL work, and we point out some benefits and challenges to obtaining student voices in SoTL. Finally, we make brief recommendations for including student voices at increasingly higher levels in SoTL work that is really all about students.

The Value of Student Involvement in Research

Very little published empirical literature exists on the value or outcomes of obtaining student voices in SoTL (exceptions include chapters in this volume). Another exception is a study by Mihans, Long, and Felten (2008) that looked at the outcomes for students involved in a course redesign team using interviews, reflective journals, and observations. Preliminary results show these students report significant new disciplinary knowledge, greater understanding about learning, the ability to effect their own learning, and increased self-efficacy in expressing their own views in an academic context. These authors argue there were also positive learning outcomes for the students taking the newly designed course.

Because of the limited literature on outcomes of student voices in SoTL, in this section we discuss some of the literature on outcomes of student involvement in research more generally. Although it is a largely unanswered empirical question, we assume some of these positive outcomes for students will hold for students engaged in SoTL research more specifically.

George Kuh (2008), drawing on years of data from the National Survey of Student Engagement and other work, discusses undergraduate research experiences as one of several educational practices that have a significant relationship to student success. Having students participate in research as part of an introductory course (e.g., General Psychology) is one way to involve students in research at a minimal level. Indeed, there is evidence that student learning and appreciation for research systematically increases in such introductory courses given that the experience is tied to specific course content and lecture material (Rosell et al., 2005).

More compelling is that exposing students to research experiences enhances learning and other positive outcomes when the course content is explicitly designed to educate learners about scholarship or research. For instance, in such courses students may be expected to participate in the design of a scholarly project/study or actually collaborate on a project or both. Others have stated that students who take such courses find them engaging, report an increased knowledge of scholarship and research, and believe they may have developed skills that are important for employment or graduate school (Wolfe, Reynolds, & Kranz, 2002). It is unlikely, however, that the experiences studied as cited here and below are SoTL projects. And, though taking the work public is a defining characteristic of SoTL, it appears that very little scholarship and research involving students in these courses reaches the public domain. In one study, less than 10% of the data gleaned from student research in such courses were published or presented outside the classroom context (Perlman & McCann, 2005).

Perhaps one of the most intriguing learning experiences for students concerns partnerships with faculty where the students can serve on a research or project team or work independently under the mentorship of a faculty member to design and implement their own research or project. Not surprisingly, when students seize such opportunities, they tend to find these experiences highly motivating and often demonstrate improvements in basic research and scholarly skills (Hunter, Laursen, & Seymour, 2007; Seymour, Hunter, Laursen, & DeAntoni, 2004). In addition, they are more likely to say they have achieved greater knowledge of research methods during their collegiate career than students who do not participate in such mentorship experiences (Zydney, Bennett, Shahid, & Bauer, 2002).

Furthermore, students who participate in such mentorship opportunities are less likely to drop out of college than students who do not participate (Nagda, Gregerman, Jonides, von Hippel, & Lerner, 1998). There is also evidence that most students indicate such experiences reaffirm their decision to pursue graduate education or may actually encourage such thinking (Lopatto, 2004). Also, students who participate in such experiences are much more likely to take their data public via publications or conference presentations than students who conduct research in the confines of a research methods class (Russell, 2005).

Finally, other positive outcomes, closely related to our institutional work at Illinois State University on promoting learner autonomy (see chapter 10), have been related to student involvement in research projects at other institutions. These gains include increases in self-confidence (Adhikari & Nolan, 2002; Hunter et al., 2007), better independent work habits, and improvements in dealing with obstacles and ambiguity (Lopatto, 2004).

Thus, there are some positive outcomes for students engaging in scholarship and research by serving in various roles. It is apparent that faculty-student research partnerships have a stronger effect on the social and academic development of the student than minor research experiences in more traditional classroom environments. Though the focus of this literature is on the position and tasks students have in sharing their voices in research, those roles also vary in the level of involvement and nature/degree of interpersonal interactions or relationships. These and other factors are likely related to the existence and extent of the positive outcomes for students. Finally, most of these studies are about student experiences with traditional disciplinary research, not SoTL, and focus on the benefits to students rather than those benefits and the value of students' voices for the research. Further research on the processes and outcomes of student voices in SoTL is needed.

A Range of Student Voices in SoTL

We present a continuum of roles students may play in SoTL and, thus, mechanisms or channels to hear student voices (see Figure 6.1). It is important to consider a wide range of ways to hear student voices, as the concept of student voices and of SoTL can be broad. The continuum of student roles in scholarly teaching and SoTL ranges from simply serving as research subjects in a SoTL study to working as an independent SoTL researcher (McKinney, 2007). As we move from left to right on the continuum of roles, the degree of student autonomy, the complexity of the tasks students are engaged in, the active nature of the work, and the connection to the instructor(s) all increase.

In terms of SoTL as formal empirical research or systematic scholarly work on teaching and learning made public (qualitative or quantitative; from a humanities/fine arts or social science or science paradigm), students may initially participate in SoTL as subject/participant giving us important data about their learning and related variables germane to our teaching-learning questions. A model that is probably familiar to many readers to obtain student involvement and voices at this level is to offer course extra credit for participation in a scholarly or research opportunity. Another model is to require students to participate in research as a mechanism to address specific course objectives. For example, a SoTL research experience may be required in an education course or disciplinary capstone course, with the expectation that students will learn more about research methods, SoTL, and/or learning in their field. Students in a class might also be required to complete an assignment (e.g., a learning log or reflective journal) that meets a learning

FIGURE 6.1

A Continuum of the Range of Student Voices in SoTL

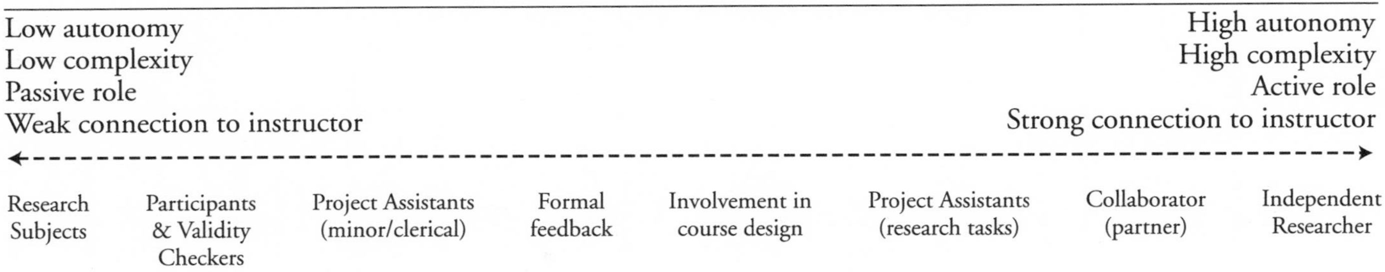

Research Subjects	Participants & Validity Checkers	Project Assistants (minor/clerical)	Formal feedback	Involvement in course design	Project Assistants (research tasks)	Collaborator (partner)	Independent Researcher

Low autonomy
Low complexity
Passive role
Weak connection to instructor

High autonomy
High complexity
Active role
Strong connection to instructor

objective of the course and is later, with appropriate institutional review board (IRB) approval, used as data in a SoTL study. Most often, however, faculty members tend to approach student participants in SoTL studies as volunteers who may benefit from the experience.

Closely related to the participant/subject-only role, especially in qualitative research, is for the participants to review the validity of an initial summary or analysis of data. For example, participants in an interview study may read the interviewer's notes or initial analysis of the interview and identify any glaring misunderstandings, errors, or omissions.

This somewhat modest role becomes more elaborate when students participate as assistants in SoTL research/scholarship. As assistants, students may be in a paid position, enrolled in a course, in a mentorship relationship with an instructor, involved in a co-curricular activity (e.g., via a department/disciplinary student organization), or in other contexts. Often students play minor assistant roles where their contributions take the form of research clerical tasks. Yet, they may also have the opportunity to express their views on, for example, the teaching-learning problem or the ideas for the creative product or the measures used in the SoTL study.

Student voices in SoTL could also include such roles as having students provide formal, systematic, interactive feedback about individual courses, the curriculum, teaching strategies, or assignments via mechanisms like classroom assessment techniques (Angelo & Cross, 1993), reflective papers, focus groups, or special seminars. A related but more complex role would be to have students play a major part in curriculum reform or the design/redesign of a course. Students, as co-presenters, could then share this work publicly at the local level or beyond through presentations or videos or papers or Web sites.

Moving to the right on our continuum in Figure 6.1, students can also engage in complex and meaningful research assistant experiences where they help with, and have voices in, tasks such as assembling questionnaire packets, gathering documents for a course portfolio, pilot testing study procedures, scheduling data collection times, conducting library work, and helping to collect or analyze data.

Students may take on the role of research partner in a formal empirical SoTL study by helping to define/refine teaching-learning questions, think about a conceptual framework, design a study or measures, write summaries of past work, collaborate on the creative product design, administer questionnaires, conduct interviews, analyze data, and so on. They can also co-author reports or papers, write reflective essays, co-present findings, develop applications of SoTL results and reflections, and help to implement applications. In other words, students can serve as full partners in co-inquiry. Finally, students may become independent SoTL researchers, seeking answers to SoTL questions they have developed and using the skills gained in their previous mentored experiences.

Examples of Student Voices in SoTL

As discussed, students can play multiple roles, from the subject of the SoTL project to conducting their own independent SoTL projects, and this wide range of voices can all benefit SoTL work. Next we offer a few concrete examples from various institutions to illustrate some of the roles discussed above. Other chapters in this book provide additional detailed examples.

Western Washington University's (WWU) Teaching-Learning Academy (TLA) is a dialogue forum to study and enhance the learning environment at WWU. This initiative includes students, faculty, staff, administrators, and community members. In addition to sponsoring all-campus events, TLA meets every other week in groups to discuss a teaching-learning question generated by the group members, including its students. Videotapes of some TLA dialogue sessions have been made public in presentations and online. For more information on the TLA, see http://www.wwu.edu/depts/tla and chapters 2 and 3 in this volume.

Instructors at Elon University hear student voices through course design efforts (e.g., Mihans et al., 2008). Seven students on a course redesign team worked with instructors to redesign an upper-level required education course. The students played a major role in all the decisions about the course through meetings, discussions, reviewing and selecting materials, and so forth. In addition, the students were involved as participants (and some of the students as research assistants) in a SoTL study of the course redesign process and its impact on learning. (See chapters 7 and 8 for other examples of course redesign with students at Elon University.)

In our internal SoTL grant program at Illinois State University, proposals must be submitted by a team of researchers, at least one of whom must be an undergraduate or graduate student. One of our anthropologists, for example, was studying the impact on learning by having students engage in ethnographies of the university. She obtained student voices by having these students share, online and in oral presentations, their ethnographies and their reflections about this learning activity. In addition she hired a student who had previously participated in the ethnography class and project to serve as her research assistant on the SoTL study of this initiative (G. Hunter & C. C. Garcia, personal communication, June 3, 2008).

Creasey, Jarvis, and Gadke (2008) conducted a funded questionnaire study assessing the role of contextual, student, and instructor variables (e.g., classroom size, student attachment, teacher immediacy) influencing achievement motivation and learner autonomy. The student member of the research team received a stipend for gathering relevant literature, piloting assessment measures, collecting data, and assisting with data analysis and interpretation. The student researcher participated in a grant recipient research circle and co-authored several related professional presentations. This same student received additional funding in another SoTL project with these researchers and has co-authored a paper that is under review by a professional journal.

Another group (Herrmann, McBride, & Zimmerman, 2009) investigated learning in undergraduate introductory psychology courses. The student member of the team (Herrmann), who is also a co-author of this chapter, offered the following summary of his experiences and their benefits to his development:

> When I was asked if I wanted to help two professors with a SoTL grant, I had no idea just how much I would gain from the experience. The semester after I had been an undergraduate teaching assistant for one of my professor's Introduction to Psychology course, she approached me and asked if I wanted to help her and another instructor of the course on a grant to assess the development of student autonomy among psychology majors. I was very interested, so I agreed and started to work with them in the summer. The following fall semester, I again was an undergraduate teaching assistant for the Introduction to Psychology course, and we collected data throughout the fall semester. During the next semester, I was responsible for entering the data into a computer account for statistical analyses. Now that the analyses are complete, we have presented the results at a local conference and are beginning to prepare a manuscript we hope to publish. I was able to work closely with these two professors and received hands-on learning about grants, teaching, and research. I am currently a graduate student in

the psychology program at Illinois State University, and I have plans of becoming a university professor. Working on this grant has helped me to really think about my learning as a student and also my teaching to undergraduate students; it has only reinforced my desire to go to graduate school and to be a professor to help students learn—and hopefully to learn better! My involvement in the SoTL grant has allowed me to not only learn more about the job of a professor, but has also helped me add invaluable credentials to my vita.

Benefits and Challenges of Student Voices in SoTL

A variety of benefits and challenges to the various ways students have voices in SoTL are discussed above. The purpose of this chapter is primarily to describe and illustrate the range of ways to obtain student voices. For a more in-depth discussion of the benefits and challenges see, for example, chapters 4 and 10. We will, however, note a few possible benefits, challenges, and tips here as well.

Mutual benefits from these collaborations include practical solutions to certain barriers to doing SoTL projects. For example, faculty members benefit from gaining economical assistance, finding partners with skills they may not have, and by alleviating time restraints. Students may earn money or credit, develop relationships with faculty members, secure letters of recommendation, and discover new self-knowledge and skills. Furthermore, working with students in SoTL efforts also provides a special and important learning opportunity that may enhance motivation and autonomy as they learn about scholarship, research, and teaching and learning. Students also can discover the depth of faculty commitment to enhancing their learning. In addition students will likely benefit from enhanced teaching and improved curricula that result from these efforts.

But, again, the real benefits for the SoTL project are the perspectives and insights students bring to SoTL. We desperately need data to confirm that including students in various phases of SoTL has the kinds of benefits we have observed in our collaborations with students: decreased ethical problems, enhanced research questions, improved project/study designs, and more meaningful interpretation of data (McKinney, 2007).

Challenges to obtaining student voices by involving students directly in SoTL include training, compensation, power relationships, and ethical issues. In terms of training, not all students in all situations will have the motivation, experiences, or skills needed to contribute to and gain from sharing their voices through such involvement. SoTL researchers must be thoughtful about how they will work with students in a given scholarly teaching or SoTL project, recruit students for such projects, train students, and supervise them. When time and resources for SoTL are limited, faculty and staff may be especially likely to see the potential practical value of student collaborators, but we must remember that training and supervision also take time and resources. Given the value of student voices, however, we believe such efforts are well worth it.

Students must also receive recognition for this work. There are several ways to compensate and reward students for sharing their voices in scholarly teaching and SoTL (McKinney, 2007). Students may participate in SoTL work for extra credit in a class and, thus, their motivation is mainly extrinsic. However, more autonomous students with intrinsic interests in SoTL generally or in the teaching-learning problem specifically may seek opportunities with faculty conducting SoTL projects. In doing so, they may gain by learning firsthand about research and scholarship, about the dedication to student learning held by SoTL researchers, and about why instructors teach the way they do, and what students are learning or how to improve learning. Other forms of compensation and recognition for students involved in SoTL are available. Students may be included in grants for SoTL projects that provide funding in terms of a stipend or travel support to professional meetings. As noted earlier, students may also receive more informative recommendation letters from faculty documenting their work as an assistant or collaborator as they move forward in their career.

The complex nature of the relationships among faculty, staff, and students can also be a challenge to listening to student voices in SoTL. In particular, there are formal power differences among these groups with students in general having less organizational (e.g., positions, status) and interpersonal (e.g., age) power than faculty and staff members. In addition, some faculty and staff may be unable to relinquish control to student collaborators. Faculty and staff must rethink these relationships and build mechanisms to promote student autonomy in this work into the structure of the collaborations.

Ethical Considerations Related to Student Voices

Related to issues of power, SoTL research raises other ethical issues that constitute another set of challenges in inviting student voices into SoTL. It was a surprise to one of our authors, who happens to be the chair of our local IRB, when some faculty members at our institution were confused about whether SoTL work needed IRB review. Some SoTL work, such as the creation of a course portfolio, a teacher's reflective essay, involving students in course assessment and design, or content analysis of existing documents of some sort, may not need IRB action. However, because SoTL projects often involve human research participants and because they are designed for generalization (publication or presentation), this work often meets the threshold for human subjects research as mandated by federal guidelines and thus needs IRB review. As with any research study, such reviews must take place before initiating participant recruitment and data collection.

Where do student researchers in any of the roles discussed above fit into the IRB process? When working on faculty SoTL research, it is customary to add students to the IRB protocol as collaborators, and students ordinarily must have their research approved by the IRB when conducting their own independent, human subjects research—including SoTL research. A small amount of student-led SoTL research could also take place within a course (e.g., education course, capstone course, methods course) where a so-called classroom research policy applies.

Institutional policies on such course-based student research vary from place to place; however, it has become increasingly common for institutions to adopt such a policy where the burden of responsibility for ethical projects is placed on the instructor who teaches his or her students research ethics and encourages them to design somewhat innocuous projects that will not be presented or published. Although the research is not submitted to the IRB for official review, generally such policies demand that the student researcher still conduct his or her work in an ethical manner (e.g., basic informed consent, protection of privacy). Because the work is not designed for generalization, an advocate of such a policy would claim that this stance saves instructor/student time and reduces the workload of often overburdened IRBs. This is problematic for SoTL work, however, in at least two ways. First, given that a defining characteristic of SoTL is that it be made public, such work would not really be SoTL but would be assessment or *practicing* research on teaching and learning rather than the scholarship of teaching and learning. Second, if students are instructed they do not need to go through the IRB process and then proceed to collect their data and later decide they want to publish or present the findings, ethically they should not do so.

Regardless of whether student SoTL projects go through an IRB review process, what ethical considerations related to obtaining student voices arise in such work? First, students may not always feel free to use their voices honestly and completely when engaged in scholarly teaching or SoTL activities. They may feel concern at harming an instructor or class with their honest views or they may experience peer pressure to express certain opinions, for example. These problems could occur in situations (design teams, focus groups, settings with powerful faculty and staff) where student voices are not anonymous.

When considering data collection in class environments—a central feature of most SoTL research—one must consider the possible dual roles that emerge for students. For example, if the classroom instructor attempts to secure consent or assist a student in data collection, it is possible that some student participants may feel coerced to consent or provide "good" data because of the power differential between themselves and the instructor. Although asking a student researcher to obtain consent and collect data without the presence of the instructor can circumvent this problem, the difficulty is not completely addressed if the student has some form of instructional role in the class (e.g., the student is a researcher and teaching assistant). In such instances, it would be advisable to ask a disinterested third party to obtain consent and collect the data.

A related difficulty is that any student researcher collecting data on students may know his or her participants. In some cases, this may not be a concern; for instance, consider the case where the student researcher happens to know a couple of students in a large class but is simply collecting data using anonymous surveys. The ante is higher, however, in cases where the student researcher can connect specific data to a friend or acquaintance. As an example, consider an audiotaped focus group that contains a participant who is a friend of the student researcher. In this case, the student researcher not only knows the student but can also tie his or her identity to the responses. At the very least, the student researcher should have training regarding confidentiality guidelines, and at the other extreme, perhaps the student participant should be asked to excuse herself or himself from the study before the informed consent process. The latter would seem to be the only option if the participants were asked to speak on controversial issues pertaining to a class or instructor.

Thus, it appears there are many possible benefits to students, their SoTL collaborators, and the SoTL projects of obtaining student voices, although empirical published research is needed on these benefits. In addition, however, challenges to obtaining and hearing student voices in SoTL include those related to training, compensation, power, and ethics.

Conclusions

We conclude this chapter by offering a few recommendations about involving students in the range of roles presented here so that we can hear the contributions from our students' voices.

- Do involve students, undergraduate and graduate, as appropriate.
- Compensate/recognize students in meaningful ways for their time and effort, but also encourage intrinsic reasons for participation.
- Attempt to involve multiple and diverse (broadly defined) students— not just academically strong students or students involved in student government or students who initially self-select, for example.
- Take the time to listen to the students about their skills and draw on the students' strengths to improve the SoTL work.
- Have students engaged in meaningful, nontrivial tasks related to SoTL projects.
- Provide opportunities for multiple students to share their ideas as well as for discussion and interaction in the process.
- Be aware of and deal with possible ethical problems related to student voices in SoTL.
- Support students in taking major responsibility in some form for making public SoTL work through performances, presentations, or publications.
- Help students see connections between SoTL projects and the implications for their own learning.
- Learn to reduce power differences and relinquish control in collaborations with students while respecting appropriate boundaries.
- Conduct and publish—with students—empirical studies of the outcomes for students, faculty, and the SoTL work of listening to student voices.

Note

1. We thank the members of our other writing team, Michael Sublett, Jeffrey Walsh, and Denise Faigao, as well as our "critical friends," Betsy Decyk, Ellen Gutman, Erin Sergison, Chelsea Martin, and Jeffrey Bernstein, for comments on earlier drafts.

References

Adhikari, N., & Nolan, D. (2002). But what good came of it at last?: How to assess the value of undergraduate research. *Notices of the AMS, 49*(10), 1252–1257.

Angelo, T. A., & Cross, K. P. (1993). *Classroom assessment techniques: A handbook for college teachers.* San Francisco: Jossey-Bass.

Creasey, G., Jarvis, P., & Gadke, D. (2008). *Student attachment stances, instructor immediacy, and student instructor relationships as predictors of achievement expectancies in college students.* Manuscript submitted for publication.

Herrmann, D., McBride, D. M., & Zimmerman, C. (2009, January). *Developing and assessing student autonomy in the first-year experience of psychology majors.* Poster session presented at the annual Teaching and Learning Symposium, Illinois State University, Normal.

Hunter, A., Laursen, S., & Seymour, E. (2007). Becoming a scientist: The role of undergraduate research in students' cognitive, personal, and professional development. *Science Education, 91*(1), 36–74.

Illinois State University. (2009). *The scholarship of teaching and learning.* Retrieved July 15, 2008, from http://www.sotl.ilstu.edu/

Kuh, G. (2008). *High-impact educational practices: What they are, who has access to them, and why they matter.* Washington, DC: Association of American Colleges and Universities.

Lopatto, D. (2004). Survey of undergraduate research experiences (SURE): First findings. *Cell Biology Education, 3*, 270–277.

McKinney, K. (2007). Enhancing learning through the scholarship of teaching and learning: The challenges and joys of juggling. Bolton, MA: Anker.

Mihans, R., Long, D., & Felten, P. (2008). Power and expertise: Student-faculty collaboration in course design and the scholarship of teaching and learning. *The International Journal of the Scholarship of Teaching and Learning, 2*(2). Retrieved July 1, 2008, from http://academics.georgiasouthern.edu/ijsotl/v2n2/essays_about_esotl/PDFs/Es say_Felten_et_al.pdf

Nagda, B., Gregerman, S., Jonides, J., von Hippel, W., & Lerner, J. (1998). Undergraduate student-faculty research partnerships affect student retention. *The Review of Higher Education, 22*, 55–72.

Perlman, B., & McCann, L. (2005). Undergraduate research experiences in psychology: A national study of courses and curricula. *Teaching of Psychology, 32,* 5–14.

Rosell, M., Beck, D., Luther, K., Goedert, K., Shore, W., & Anderson, D. (2005). The pedagogical value of experimental participation paired with course content. *Teaching of Psychology, 32,* 95–99.

Russell, S. H. (2005). *Evaluation of NSF Support for undergraduate research opportunities: Survey of STEM graduates.* Arlington, VA: National Science Foundation.

Seymour, E., Hunter, A., Laursen, S., & DeAntoni, T. (2004). Establishing the benefits of research experiences for undergraduates in the sciences: First findings from a three-year study. *Science Education, 88*(4), 493–534.

Wolfe, C., Reynolds, B., & Kranz, J. (2002). A care for undergrad labs. *APS Observer, 15,* 7–8.

Zydney, A., Bennett, J., Shahid, A., & Bauer, K. (2002). Faculty perspectives regarding an undergraduate research experience in science and engineering. *Journal of Engineering Education, 91,* 291–297.

7

EQUALIZING VOICES

Student-Faculty Partnership in Course Design

Ayesha Delpish, Alexa Darby, Ashley Holmes, Mary Knight-McKenna, Richard Mihans, Catherine King, and Peter Felten

T his chapter describes a particular approach to the scholarship of teaching and learning (SoTL)—integrating student, faculty, and community voices in the course design process to explore fundamental teaching and learning problems from multiple perspectives. This approach has potential for significant new insights to improve teaching and learning in individual courses and to contribute to scholarly discourse about collaboration in teaching and learning.

We faculty describe four specific cases with varied processes and participants, but all including students (see Appendix 7.A). The starting point of each case was a significant teaching problem the instructor(s) chose to treat as an object of scholarly inquiry (Bass, 1999) rather than as simply a mistake to be fixed. In each case, the problem resided in the overall design of the course, which Fink (2003) has argued is "the most significant bottleneck to better teaching and learning in higher education" (p. 24). Each case tells a story of the importance of negotiating the significant institutional and interpersonal issues of voice, expertise, and power to represent the perspectives of multiple stakeholders and provide opportunities for critique, comparison, and pursuit of scholarly inquiries in ways that an instructor working alone could not achieve.

Example Number 1: Redesigning a "Broken" Course

RICHARD MIHANS[1]

This project emerged from a common teaching problem—a basic mismatch between faculty and student perceptions of a course. Elon University's Department of Education curriculum included a required course in classroom management. Faculty believed the course to be vital for the success of beginning elementary and middle school teachers, but students often complained that the course was irrelevant and unnecessary

Rather than ignore the students or change the curriculum, two faculty members (Mihans and Long) decided to ask students for help in reinventing this broken course. When we proposed this approach to all education majors, the students responded enthusiastically. We then asked for applications from students who would like to join a Course Redesign Design Team (CRDT) that would meet twice weekly during the January term of 2006. The CRDT would develop new course objectives, choose a suitable textbook, align assignments with course goals and objectives, and do miscellaneous tasks associated with developing a course. We also asked Peter Felten, director of Elon's Center for the Advancement of Teaching and Learning, to join the CRDT to mediate any potential conflicts that might arise from the inherently asymmetrical power relationships between professors and students.

The seven students selected to join the CRDT were undergraduate elementary education majors in their junior or senior years. Some of them had taken the course to be redesigned, while others had not yet enrolled in it.

The CRDT held eight 2-hour meetings during January, and participants completed 25 hours of work outside the meetings. Student participants received a stipend, paid by the Center for the Advancement of Teaching and Learning, so that they could focus on the CRDT as their "job" during that term. The entire team kept journals about our experiences, as well as participated in three taped interviews about the process and our experiences (pre-, during, and post-CRDT).

We (Deborah Long and I) were tempted to develop the new course objectives prior to the first team meeting, believing that the students, as novices in the field of education, would not be able to effectively contribute to this essential first step in course design. How could they be expected to know what future students should gain from taking the course? However, after considerable discussion, we realized that beginning the process without student voices would defeat the project's purpose. We had to adjust to sharing power in the CRDT even before the first meeting occurred by adjusting our mind-set and deliberately resisting making final decisions without the input of our student partners. Therefore, all instructional decisions resulted from the group's meetings.

Students on the team also had to adjust to the new power dynamics. The turning point for them came after a collaborative process of drafting the course objectives when we focused on selecting a course textbook. We had identified 25 possible books, deliberately casting a wide net to allow maximum student voice in the selection process. The CRDT decided that each student member of the team would rate several books on a scale developed by the team that included alignment with course objectives, readability, appropriateness for audience, and overall quality.

When the CRDT next discussed the books, the group decided we would automatically exclude texts receiving low ratings from multiple reviewers (most texts were reviewed by two students). These cuts surprised and delighted the student members of the team because we excluded books (including a text used in the past) without any objections from Deborah or me. Once the options had been narrowed, members of the CRDT again reviewed the options—this time we also rated each book. Although we faculty ultimately preferred a more theoretical text, in the end the CRDT selected a practical text supplemented with readings that addressed theory. The textbook selection process dramatically shifted the dynamics in the CRDT, as students developed a sense of their own individual and collective voices and power in the process. After the initial textbook cuts, students on the team became much more willing to disagree with us and with each other.

When the course redesign process concluded, the whole group felt extremely proud because we had all taken ownership of the decision. We faculty had become more willing to trust student partners by sharing power with them, not exerting it over them. After all, the students possessed real expertise and insight into the expectations and needs of future students who would take this course. As faculty, however, we did not abdicate responsibility for their course; instead, we used their expertise about the knowledge and skills students would need to develop in the course to guide the redesign process. This partnership was a sharing of power in the truest sense.

Analysis of the CRDT participant interviews and journals demonstrated that the collaborative process not only produced an effective new course (as seen in higher evaluations than in previous terms) but also produced significant learning for everyone on the team. Students on the team gained significant new disciplinary knowledge; developed what Hutchings (2005) calls *pedagogical intelligence*, an understanding about how learning happens; and became more competent and confident in expressing their own expertise in academic settings. We also changed, learning the value of really listening to students. We now teach all our courses somewhat differently because we are more attuned to student needs and to the expertise students themselves bring to the table. We have wholeheartedly embraced the concept of student collaboration in course design and have witnessed how student empowerment can lead to increased motivation and participation and improved problem-solving skills (Haynes, 2001). As one of the team students said in an interview: "Even in college, even now, I think some teachers . . . are so focused on getting stuff done that they don't pay attention to their students, who I think are the most valuable resources [in a classroom]." In our case, we faculty learned to pay close attention to our students as invaluable resources for improving our classes.

Example Number 2: Undergraduate Research Extending Into SoTL

Alexa Darby and Mary Knight-McKenna

Critical reflection and problem solving around effective instructional practices are central to the work of teacher education programs. This orientation lends itself naturally to the incorporation of SoTL into teacher education. Like the previous SoTL project, this example occurred in courses that prepare future teachers. Unlike the first example, which involved a cadre of students working with professors for 1 month to redesign a course, this one occurred over a 2-year period with one undergraduate research student.

We organized discussion of this SoTL example around three key points. The first relates to the pedagogical challenges of preparing preservice teachers for possible employment in high-poverty schools, where their backgrounds are often widely different from the diverse students they encounter. The second key point relates to the challenge of mentoring an undergraduate student in the research process. The third main point illustrates the undergraduate's challenge to develop as a SoTL researcher. This case study highlights a turning point for a novice researcher in becoming an equal partner in a SoTL project.

Pedagogical Challenge

High-poverty schools have an ongoing need to recruit and retain highly qualified teachers. Because of low teacher salaries, difficult working conditions, and the challenges of teaching diverse populations these schools are known as *hard-to-staff* schools (Berry, 2004). Research has indicated that when preservice teachers initially work with individuals whose ethnic and socioeconomic backgrounds are different from theirs, stereotypes are reinforced, not changed (Conchran-Smith, 1991).

Negative stereotyping is frequently an issue in this situation, and faculty in teacher education programs struggle with the questions of how to reduce stereotypical thinking. Academic service learning (ASL) is one pedagogy approach known to facilitate students' understanding of diversity (Eyler & Giles, 1999; Nicholas, Harwood, & Radoff, 2007; Root, Callahan, & Sepanski, 2002; Taylor & Trepanier-Street, 2007). There has been an increased use of ASL in teacher education courses (Anderson & Erickson, 2003). This SoTL project originated when a teacher educator (Knight-McKenna) and an educational psychologist (Darby) made the decision to research the use of ASL with the goal of increasing the interest of our middle- to upper-class preservice teachers for teaching in high-poverty schools. Given the complexity of the research question and the amount of data collection and analysis required, we welcomed the assistance of an undergraduate researcher.

The results of our initial research on the preservice teachers' ASL experience showed that a large portion of the preservice teachers still engaged in negative stereotyping when discussing their experiences in high-poverty schools. The continued use of stereotypes was distressing; we grappled with the meanings and implications of the outcomes and brainstormed ways to address this concern with our undergraduate research partner. Our goal was to have students move beyond their stereotypes to a better understanding and appreciation of diversity.

With the help of our student partner, we redesigned our course to employ several instructional strategies to meet our goal. For example, we devoted one class period to helping students examine their expectations of school. We asked the students to list their expectations of students, parents, and teachers. The research student analyzed the results, finding that 97% of the preservice teachers' expectations were based on their own school experiences. This finding prompted a discussion with the students about the expectations they bring with them into high-poverty schools and what this means for the judgments they make as they work in these schools. With our research student's assistance, we helped the students more successfully meet this course goal.

Mentoring Challenge

In addition to our goal of determining the effectiveness of specific ASL courses, we also entered this project with the goal of training a budding researcher. Prior to this research project, the undergraduate psychology student we selected had taken a research course but needed very clear scaffolding and specific direction on the research process. In weekly team meetings, we used the apprenticeship model of situation learning known as *legitimate peripheral participation* (Lave & Wenger, 1991). At first the research student had very little power in the process, playing a peripheral role in its direction and participating mostly by completing assigned tasks. Under our faculty guidance, the student moved along Willison and O'Regan's (2007) trajectory of research development. She began at Level I, needing guidance and structure, and over the course of 2 years, progressed to Level III, working independently and involving faculty only as needed.

Despite the challenges we encountered as faculty mentors, we were convinced of the numerous benefits. The literature shows, and our experience supports, undergraduate students who participate in research for a semester or more leave their college experience with stronger critical thinking skills, communication skills, enhanced self-efficacy, and clarification of career goals (Bauer & Bennett, 2003; Kinkead, 2003; Seymour, Hunter, Laursen, & DeAntoni, 2004; Willison & O'Regan, 2007). Also, students who participate in undergraduate research are twice as likely to successfully pursue a doctoral degree as students who do not participate in an undergraduate research experience (Bauer & Bennett).

Development Challenge

Throughout the process, the undergraduate research student saw us wrestling with a large societal issue that had no ready answers. These authentic discussions, uncharacteristic of typical student-faculty interactions, created the opportunity for the research student to have a stronger voice. The undergraduate research student increasingly participated in all phases of the course redesign and collected and analyzed data to assess the effectiveness of the new instructional practices. This sense of equalization of power enhanced her motivation and she became a legitimate, central participant in the research team (Lave & Wenger, 1991).

During the brainstorming phase, we presented our results at a statewide ASL conference. This experience of co-presenting enhanced her role as a full member of the research team. Just prior to graduation, a fellow psychology student interviewed the research student about her experiences on the research team. In this interview she stated,

> I would say that after the [ASL] conference . . . I felt like I had much more power to help with the research project and slowly I in turn participated more. By the end of the project I felt much more confident and in control of what was going on and I felt like my participation was important, I was almost like a co-researcher. We always discussed everything that we were doing and especially in the latter part of the research, I felt like I had a very equal voice in it.

In the interview, she also said,

> I feel like I've had a lot of involvement, which is kind of surprising since I have no idea how to teach a classroom or anything like that. But just knowing what our research has found and being the student, being in classes all the time, I guess. You know, I have a completely different perspective than the two professors would, who are the people doing instruction for the students. So I . . . could talk about different activities that were most interesting and that students would get the most value out of. So that was helpful.

As she neared graduation, we acknowledged the research student's valuable contribution to the team, based not only on her newly acquired research skills but also on her thorough grasp of the research findings and her learner expertise. She helped us understand the need for instructional change that would bring about a shift in preservice teachers' expectations in high-poverty schools.

While this particular example deals with a critical issue in the field of education, the process of extending undergraduate research into SoTL is applicable to a variety of fields. The authentic nature of this process is portrayed in the research student's concluding comments:

> And there's actually a purpose to our research instead of just doing research to find out results. We actually are doing research to make a difference in people's lives. . . . So being able to apply our findings to a real-world classroom setting is the next [step], but a lot of undergraduate researchers just do the research, have the findings, and write the paper, and don't get to do that next step, even if that's really important. That's the whole reason you do research.

Example Number 3: Community and Student Voices in the Course Redesign Process

Ashley Holmes

College Writing at Elon University is a course that nearly all students are required to take in the fall or spring of their 1st year. The College Writing course I first taught in spring 2007 incorporated a minimum 20-hour service requirement to be completed outside class time. The students' semester-long service experiences at community agencies became the *text* for the course, providing the subject and exigencies for their compositions; students composed a series of four assignments that fell into Thomas Deans's (2000) categories of writing *about* and *for* the community.

As Bass (1999) so aptly describes, teaching can be filled with crises and pitfalls. My first attempt at teaching a composition course with an ASL component was not entirely successful. Rather than giving up or treating the difficult aspects of the class as problems to be fixed, like Bass I chose to view the ending as a new beginning. As the semester of my ASL course drew to a close, I considered ways to investigate the problems my students, community partners, and I had encountered. I designed a SoTL project, similar to the first case described in this chapter, as a way of gathering feedback from students and the community to enhance the ASL course for future semesters. The success of the project relied on a crucial component—my commitment to listen to and incorporate the voices of students and the community.

I asked three former students, as well as one of the six community leaders my students served with, to join me in the process of making curricular decisions about the course that I would again teach the following spring; the five of us constituted the CRDT. The three student members were females who took my course as second-semester 1st-year students and joined the CRDT as sophomores the following fall. The community partner was the founding director of a local nonprofit organization that provides "therapeutic horseback riding, recreational therapy, animal-assisted therapy, and horticulture therapy to individuals with or without disabilities" (Kopper Top Life Learning Center, 2008).

The CRDT met in four 2-hour meetings during the fall 2007 semester. In the spirit of equal partnership, we scheduled two of the course redesign meetings on campus and two at the community partner site. Each participant received a modest stipend for her participation and lunch at each of the meetings, funded by a small grant from Elon University.

Much like the first case example in this chapter, the work of the CRDT followed the framework of Wiggins and McTighe's (2005) *Understanding by Design*. Unlike the first case, students in this CRDT were not building the course from the ground up because the university's writing program predetermined the course goals. However, the CRDT did play a major role in determining the course activities that would best facilitate the learning goals, particularly in an ASL course context. In short, the goals of the CRDT were to

1. Increase communication among students, faculty, and community partners.
2. Reconceptualize and enhance the course assignments and service components.

The CRDT project worked from the premise that each participant brought a distinctive expertise and standpoint to the course redesign process. Standpoint theorists argue that knowledge is socially situated and that research should be grounded in and give value to the experiences of voiceless or oppressed groups (Harding, 2004; Hartsock, 1997; Orbe, 1998). The work of the CRDT used standpoint theory as a framework, and my hypothesis was that the multiple standpoints from students, the community partner, and the instructor during the course redesign process would enhance the curriculum.

My commitment to give voice to and acknowledge each participant's experiences with ASL guided the activities of CRDT; nonetheless, this process called for a series of negotiations when considering course changes. An example of this negotiation occurred in our extended discussions about the required number of service hours for the course. After one student suggested 20 hours was a fair minimum requirement, a second student asserted that some may want to complete more than the minimum hours. She proposed that for 40 hours of service, students should receive extra credit equivalent to an A on a paper.

The community partner agreed with the students about the extra credit. As the instructor, my initial response was, "I don't really do extra credit." I thought that it was unfair to weigh extra hours as heavily as a major course assignment. The standpoint I contributed to the group considered the goals and assignments from the course at a broad level; I also brought to the table my expertise in teaching writing. As I discussed the suggested change from my standpoint, I asserted that 1 hour of service was not equivalent to the amount of time, effort, and course-based skills required of obtaining an A on an essay. However, for the team members' suggestions to be legitimately valued, I listened and worked toward finding a compromise. Responding to my concerns, the students suggested the option of dropping a lowest quiz grade or skipping a homework assignment in exchange for extra service hours; this was a change I knew I could comfortably incorporate. As this example shows, listening to students and community voices did not mean abandoning my beliefs about sound pedagogy; however, it did require that I reconsider and shift some of those beliefs.

A similar situation arose when I asked the CRDT to consider a penalty for students who did not meet the 20-hour service requirement. One student team member suggested a graduated deduction in grade depending on how many hours were short.

> I think it should be kind of like if you . . . were supposed to get 20, and you got 18, okay, you didn't get all of them, but you obviously tried, so there's a deduction off your grade, but not substantial. . . . If you did all your hours you get a 100, . . . if you get 18, say you get a couple points off, and once you drop down to 15, you get more points off, . . . and if you're under 12 or 15 then you shouldn't get any, but I think if you're kind of close, then . . .

After some discussion, the CRDT agreed that the basic premise of this policy seemed fair. This student's suggestion of a points system based on degrees of completion marked a significant and needed change to the course policy. My previous all-or-nothing policy did not account for, as this CRDT participant notes, a student who completed less than 20 hours but still came close. When I taught the course again in the spring, I took these suggestions of the CRDT group including the points system and the potential for extra credit. By the end of the meetings, the CRDT suggested several additional changes, which I made when I taught it in spring 2008. These changes included a reduction in the number of community agencies, opportunities for students to visit other agencies, adoption of a new textbook, and major changes in the nature of the course assignments.

Though the original intent of the CRDT's work was to enhance course experiences for *future* students, the team members themselves benefitted from being part of the redesign process. One benefit resulted from extended time for reflection on our experiences with ASL, teaching, writing, and partnerships. For the students, the CRDT meetings prompted them to articulate their learning in new ways and to recall important course concepts such as rhetoric and audience. In addition to time for reflection, each member listened to and gained a new understanding of the others' social standpoints. For instance, when one student shared her story of getting lost the first time driving to the service site, I (as the instructor) better understood her position of having to manage the course service experiences. Additionally, when the community partner shared stories of her frustration with students from other courses failing to show up for service hours, I—as well as the student participants—gained a new appreciation for the sacrifices community members make when they agree to work with the university in ASL. Finally, in explaining the work involved in planning and grading and the additional workload of designing and teaching 1st-year composition as an ASL course, the students and the community partner gained a greater understanding of the work of professors in the academy.

The CRDT reconvened for a final meeting in spring 2008 to reflect on the group's process and accomplishments. For the community partner, increased communication was a major benefit resulting from the CRDT experiences; she commented: "I really felt more connected. I think it was more beneficial. If other professors hear that, then maybe they would be more receptive to it. Just the communication. That was a major issue." The student participants commented on how the CRDT meetings prompted them to recall how much they learned from the course service experiences. One student claimed that without the meetings, "I don't think I would have realized everything I learned"; another student participant agreed that as a result of the CRDT meetings, "We just realized how much we learned."

Example Number 4: Equalizing Voices *During* the Course

AYESHA DELPISH

While the previous cases involved collaboration between students and faculty outside the classroom, the final SoTL example involves course design involving all the enrolled students while the course was in progress. What really distinguishes this example from the others is that *current* students were given equal voices in all aspects of the course—structure, content, and assessment.

The course in question is a second-level statistics course that incoming 1st-year students take primarily to satisfy their core mathematics requirement. The main goal of most core courses in mathematics is to improve the student's quantitative reasoning skills; therefore, the class focuses as much on developing thinking processes as covering math content. Most students approach math courses with dread because they do not see the relevance to their intended major. Their prior exposure to mathematics courses usually involved continuously working similar problems until they had mastered the problem-solving technique.

To combat the typical *rote calculation* approach to statistics, I use case studies as a teaching tool, an approach that is not widely used to teach undergraduate courses in the mathematical sciences. Using the case study method allows me to expose students to a series of real-world cases that require them to work in groups to solve problems. I believe that providing situations where students can explore their own knowledge and prove/disprove their preconceived notions of *what is* stimulates their learning. The case study–based course structure allows for a unique partnership between me and each student in the class, providing students opportunities to contribute their distinctive voices to the operation of the course and to help design the learning environment to best suit those learning needs. Marzano and colleagues (1988) contend that "thinking processes often begin with an unresolved problem, a need, or an indeterminate situation. . . . The teacher's challenge is to see opportunities for using thinking processes to enhance student learning in any content area, teaching the component thinking skills as necessary" (p. 89).

The case study approach also allows for greater risk taking in terms of the course design. In general, students do not learn course content prior to starting a case nor is there a definitive order for covering the material. For example, during one particular case, the fall course content sequence was one-sample tests, two-sample tests, and analysis of variance, while in the spring semester the same case resulted in a content sequence of two-sample tests, multiple regression, and analysis of variance. To a large extent, students determined the course content based on questions they compose as they work to solve the cases. I provide guidance based on observations of students working in groups as well as student feedback in the form of short papers and reflections. This guidance component is important because as Hutchings (2005) notes, it is "difficult . . . for students to reflect on and assess their own experiences as learners, to get past the idea of learning as something that happens to them (or not), to see their education as something they can create and control" (p. 1). By opening negotiations with the students from the 1st day of the course, I was able to create an environment where power could be genuinely shared. For example, any question raised by a student during class went back to the entire group with a simple *What do you all think and why?* All stakeholders made every class-level decision after discussing different possibilities.

Designing a class with an open-ended, student-driven structure requires solving many issues. Perhaps the most daunting is the apparent reduction in the instructor's power, a decrease manifested in three ways: shared course decision making; a willingness to say *I don't know* and mean it; and allowing different student groups to cover the material at different rates. Instructors might experience this reduction in power as a perceived loss of control. In traditional classroom settings, teachers act as authoritative figures who *tell* the students what they need to know, when they are going to know it, and how they are going to know it. Teachers have the final say in every decision and need to know everything about the assignments a priori. Not only did I have to deliberately share control of the course with the students in terms of decisions about content, structure, and assessments, but because of the complexity of the cases involved I had to openly admit when I did not know the solution to the problem the students were working on. I had to be willing to say *I don't know* and really mean it. My willingness to do so was terribly frustrating to some students at first as it challenged their perceptions of power in the classroom. The challenge for me then became one of being openly vulnerable while maintaining students' respect for me as their instructor.

Group pacing also presented a challenge to the instructor's power. Particularly at the beginning of the course, I encouraged groups to remain fluid, shifting membership at their discretion. I believed that this fluidity would allow students to eventually find group members whose learning styles and teaching styles were more in line with their own. I observed that in general visual learners tended to flock together, while those seeking more theoretical approaches also tended to group. However, based in part on this division, groups tended to work at different paces and pose different questions so that groups were sometimes heading in opposing directions. Each group's needs were different. This variance increased the pressure for me because students needed some question-asking skills and were not always ready at the same time.

The perceived loss of control issue was also complicated by the fact that I was the only expert on statistical analysis in the community. This gap in expertise posed some initial difficulty because my views were at times not in line with those of the students. In some instances, students challenged my a priori decisions to the point where I was tempted to fall back into the traditional role and simply say, *Because I said so!* Keeping a teaching journal and reflecting on where breakdowns occurred helped me challenge my own beliefs and reevaluate my commitment to my stated philosophy of teaching. For example, one semester the class included a module where students collected data on the drinking habits of their peers and compared their results to the university's research on this topic. I conceived the module as one that small groups would approach (like the other case studies) with group presentations at the end. However, when I proposed the assignment to the class, they voted for one large group project and presentation. While I openly voiced my concerns over 33 students working on one project together (such as individuals not pulling their weight), I was the lone voice, so they vetoed me. My reflections that night included:

> I don't think this group project will work. I really should have put my foot down and told them that my way was the only way to do it to ensure that everyone contributed. . . . some of them will simply blow it off and the importance of this module will be lost. . . . some of them are just looking for a way to do the least amount of work possible. . . . Grading this is

going to be a nightmare—should I even bother? How would I differentiate between students. . . . I should not have given them this option—it will be a disaster!

Much to my surprise, on the day of the class presentation for the alcohol module, I arrived to find each student professionally dressed with well-defined roles that allowed each person to contribute. The overall project presentation was more complete than any student effort I have ever seen—they hit all the right points and appropriately used the data to substantiate their arguments. They seemed to have developed some system that allowed everyone to apply individual strengths to the collective product—it was quite impressive. That night I noted in my journal:

> The group presentation went really well. I spoke to [student A] and [student B] after class and they told me that while there were disagreements at first, people quickly fell into different groups and assignments were made based on strengths. . . . Because they had worked with each other for 2 months now, they seem to be aware of each other's strengths and weaknesses. . . . If this happens again, be sure to have them add a component to their reflections talking about the group dynamics.

So in the end, had I resorted to a *Because I said so!* approach, I would have missed out on observing the students successfully function as a community of learners.

The fact that the students had an equal voice not only in the content and structure of the course but also in the assessments raised many issues about student grades and motivation. I found that students who took the course in the fall were generally new 1st-year students who tended to look to me for cues, perhaps because they were novices in the college environment. They also tended to focus initially on what was required to get a good grade and were very uncomfortable making decisions that would affect their grades. Students in the spring on the other hand were seasoned college students, sophomores and juniors, and seemed to be more open to taking risks with their assignment choices and weights. There was definitely a stronger sense that the students in the fall were motivated by grades while in the spring there was a greater interest in the pursuit of knowledge—a teacher's dream. While students in both semesters eventually took ownership of the course, the spring students achieved their comfort level faster.

Involving current students in course redesign while the course is in progress has many advantages. The *redesign as you go* approach allowed me to examine systematically the case study method of teaching statistics and the connections between power and motivation in my classroom. Students had the opportunity to have significant control over their own learning as they negotiated complex mathematical content, prompting them not only to learn math but also to develop metacognitively. By allowing student voices to run throughout the course and providing an authentic collaborative environment, the students and I all learned to adapt and develop as learners.

Conclusion

Equalizing faculty and student voices proved to be difficult in all four cases examined here. Students are accustomed to, and often comfortable with, assuming a relatively powerless role in the classroom, just as faculty are trained to believe that their disciplinary expertise gives them complete authority over the learning process. When faculty or students challenge these habits, students and faculty must confront fundamental questions about the nature of teaching and learning.

The course design process offers an opportunity to challenge those habits and ask important questions in a collaborative and scholarly environment. The cases above demonstrate that thoughtful partnership during the design process can lead not only to more effective courses and deeper student learning, but also to new insights into learning and teaching for students and faculty.

While collaborative course design may not be appropriate in all contexts, it can be powerful when the timing is right and the necessary institutional support is available. We recommend choosing collaborative partners carefully, with a clear understanding of the expertise and motivations each brings to the process. And although advance planning and close attention to the process is crucial, a genuinely open attitude is equally important. As these descriptions make clear, collaborative course design is complex and fraught with issues of voice, expertise, and power. In each case we were able to document turning points in the design process when faculty had to step back to allow the students and community partner to step forward to make significant contributions. Faculty and students beginning collaborative design efforts should strive to anticipate and seize such moments when the equalizing of voices makes transformational learning possible for all partners in the process.

Note

1. This section is adapted from Mihans, Long, and Felten (2008).

References

Anderson, J. F., & Erickson, J. (2003, summer). Service-learning in preservice teacher education. *Academic Exchange Quarterly, 7*(2), 111–115.

Bass, R. (1999). The scholarship of teaching: What's the problem? *Inventio, 1*(1). Retrieved August 13, 2008, from http://www.doiiit.gmu.edu/Archives/feb98/randybass.htm

Bauer, K. W., & Bennett, J. S. (2003). Alumni perceptions used to assess undergraduate research experience. *The Journal of Higher Education, 74*, 210–230.

Berry, B. (2004). Recruiting and retaining board-certified teachers for hard-to-staff schools. *NASSP Bulletin, 88*(638), 5–27.

Conchran-Smith, M. (1991). Reinventing student teaching. *Journal of Teacher Education, 42*, 104–118.

Deans, T. (2000). *Writing partnerships: Service-learning in composition.* Urbana, IL: National Council of Teachers of English.

Eyler, J., & Giles, D. E., Jr. (1999). *Where's the learning in service-learning?* San Francisco: Jossey-Bass.

Fink, L. D. (2003). *Creating significant learning experiences: An integrated approach to designing college courses.* San Francisco: Jossey-Bass.

Harding, S. (Ed.) (2004). Introduction: Standpoint theory as a site of political, philosophic, and scientific debate. In S. Harding, *The feminist standpoint theory reader: Intellectual and political controversies* (pp. 1–16). New York: Routledge.

Hartsock, N. M. (1997). The feminist standpoint: Developing the ground for a specifically feminist historical materialism. In L. Nicholson (Ed.), *The second wave: A reader in feminist theory* (pp. 216–240). New York: Routledge.

Haynes, A. (2001). Student empowerment: Student-designed syllabus: A group exercise. In K. McKinney, F. D. Beck, & B. S. Heyl (Eds.), *Sociology through active learning: Student exercises* (pp. 215–220). Thousand Oaks, CA: Pine Forge Press.

Hutchings, P. (2005, January). Building pedagogical intelligence. *Carnegie Perspectives.* Retrieved July 8, 2008, from http://www.carnegiefoundation.org/perspectives/sub.asp?key=245& subkey=571

Kinkead, J. (2003). *Valuing and supporting undergraduate research.* San Francisco: Jossey-Bass.

Kopper Top Life Learning Center. Retrieved September 1, 2008, from http://www.koppertop.org/

Lave, J., & Wenger, E. (1991). *Situated learning: Legitimate peripheral participation.* Cambridge, UK: Cambridge University Press.

Marzano, R. J., Brandt, R., Hughes, C., Jones, B., Presseisen, B., Rankin, S., & Suhor, C. (1988). Dimensions of thinking: A framework for curriculum and instruction. In A. Costa (Ed.), *Developing minds: A resource book for teaching thinking* (Vol. 1, pp. 89–93). Alexandria, VA: Association for Supervision and Curriculum Development.

Mihans, R. M., Long, D. T., & Felten, P. (2008). Power and expertise: Student-faculty collaboration in course-design and the scholarship of teaching and learning. *International Journal for the Scholarship of Teaching and Learning, 2*(2), 1–9. Retrieved January 20, 2009, from http://academics.georgiasouthern.edu/ijsotl/v2n2.html

Nicholas, J., Harwood, A. M., & Radoff, S. (2007, October). *Civic problem-solving: Results of a mentoring project with at-risk middle school students.* Paper presented at the Annual International Conference on Service-Learning Research, Tampa, FL.

Orbe, M. P. (1998). *Constructing co-cultural theory: An explication of culture, power, and communication.* Thousand Oaks, CA: Sage.

Root, S., Callahan, J., & Sepanski, J. (2002). Building teaching dispositions and service-learning practice: A multi-site study. *Michigan Journal of Community Service Learning, 8,* 50–60.

Seymour, E., Hunter, A., Laursen, S., & DeAntoni, T. (2004). Establishing the benefits of research experiences for undergraduates in the sciences: First findings from a three-year study. *Science Education, 88,* 493–534.

Taylor, J. A., & Trepanier-Street, M. (2007). Civic education in multicultural contexts: New findings from a national study. *The Social Studies, 98,* 14–18.

Wiggins, J., & McTighe, J. (2005). *Understanding by design.* Upper Saddle River, NJ: Pearson Education.

Willison, J., & O'Regan, K. (2007). Commonly known, commonly not known, totally unknown: A framework for students becoming researchers. *Higher Education Research & Development, 26,* 393–409.

APPENDIX 7.A
The Four Cases Summarized

	Course(s)	Problem	Partners	Process/Timing	Product
1.	Third-year undergraduate education major requirement	Students' belief that class is irrelevant	Two education faculty who will teach the course; seven junior or senior education majors who will *not* take the revised course; director of teaching and learning center	Biweekly meetings for 5 weeks before the new course begins	Revised course syllabus
2.	Second-year undergraduate education major requirements in psychology and education	Students maintain stereotypical beliefs despite courses	Two faculty (psychology and education) who teach the courses; one undergraduate research student	Two-year undergraduate research project	New instructional strategies
3.	First-year undergraduate required writing course	Service learning complicates nature of the course	The faculty member who teaches the course; three 2nd-year undergraduates who had taken the course; one community partner who worked with the students and instructor in the course	Four meetings before the new course begins and one midsemester meeting during implementation of the revised course	Revised course syllabus, service expectations, and assignments
4.	First-year undergraduate advanced statistics course	Students often do not see course as relevant	The faculty member teaching and the 33 students enrolled in the course	Throughout the semester as the course is occurring	Class policies, sequence of case studies, and assessment

8

BEEN THERE, DONE THAT, STILL DOING IT

Involving Students in Redesigning a Service-Learning Course

Jessie L. Moore, Lindsey Altvater, Jillian Mattera, and Emily Regan

After teaching an Introduction to Teaching English to Speakers of Other Languages (TESOL) course for four semesters, Jessie (the faculty member on our team) wanted to redesign the course to more systematically and extensively integrate a required service learning component. Jessie strongly believes that service learning enables TESOL students to observe how TESOL theories and best practices apply to real classroom contexts; furthermore, service learning enables TESOL students to help address a growing area of need in the local community. Jessie previously had worked with other former TESOL students on identifying strategies for the service learning project (Kapper, Clapp, & Lefferts, 2007), but this prior consultation had not addressed how *best* to integrate the service learning component into the overall class structure. Based on TESOL students' informal feedback, she sensed they were encountering a lot more TESOL theory, research, and practice in their service learning placements than what previously came into play in class sessions. In this chapter, we—a faculty member and undergraduate English teacher licensure students (students preparing to teach high school English)—describe how we collaborated to redesign the course to better tap those placement experiences. We also share our stories about the challenges and rewards of faculty and students working together to enhance student learning.

Since its inception at Elon University, Introduction to TESOL has included a service learning component. What started as a once-a-semester visit to local English as a Second Language (ESL) classrooms quickly grew to semester-long service learning placements with students volunteering weekly and ultimately creating curricular materials for their cooperating teachers and the ESL students.[1] While we all recognized the promise of service learning field experience, Jessie worried, and some of our experiences confirmed, that we were not realizing the full potential of this experiential learning. We had two distinct experiences—one in our TESOL class and one volunteering in ESL classrooms—and we were struggling to make connections between the two contexts while balancing our learning goals and the ESL teachers' needs.

Jessie had heard several colleagues talk about course redesign projects they pursued with students (see chapter 7), which inspired her to invite several former students to help her redesign the TESOL course. Jessie invited select students from two previous sections of the course to participate. Although she tried to recruit a diverse representation of former students, she also wanted to invite students who had been reliable participants in the sections, especially in regard to the service learning requirement and therefore could comment and reflect on how that component might more consistently and methodically inform class discussions. Seven students of the fourteen she invited responded to Jessie's initial inquiry, expressing their interest in participating in the course redesign. Another indicated his interest but asked for an alternate way to participate since he was studying abroad, and a few students volunteered to respond to survey questions—if used—but did not have time to meet because they were student teaching.

Based on students' schedules at the end of the semester, Jessie met with one group of four students over morning coffee and one group of three students over lunch. Jessie prepared a list of questions to guide the discussions but did not force the conversation to stay centered on those questions, preferring to see how the conversation developed as students recalled important classroom and service learning experiences that informed what they remembered about the course content and design. Jessie audiotaped both conversations so she and the students could refer to them while negotiating the rest of the course redesign process.

After examining students' initial feedback and the goals of the course, Jessie drafted a new syllabus and schedule that reflected students' suggestions. She then e-mailed these materials to the students for additional feedback. While other Elon faculty involved students more extensively throughout their redesign processes—even asking students to select readings, for example—the drafting and feedback cycle worked better in this case given time limitations. Furthermore, although Long and Mihans's students received course credit and a stipend for their participation (see chapter 7), course credit or monetary rewards were not an option for this project. Therefore, Jessie carefully monitored the workload of the students who also simultaneously were completing end-of-semester assignments and then starting summer jobs.

Each of us had clear motivations for participating in the course design process, though, and these motivations drove our willingness to devote time to the project. Jessie explained early that she wanted to facilitate enduring understandings of key TESOL topics and sensed that the service learning component of the course could be strengthened to better meet that goal. Jill and Emily explained their decisions to participate as follows:

> *Jill*: I really enjoyed learning the material and gaining the experience I had during my time in the TESOL course and I simply wanted to make it better for those to come. I had felt really strongly about certain aspects of the course upon its completion so I was more than willing to give my opinion when asked for it.
>
> *Emily*: Giving as much input as I can into the redesign of the TESOL class will hopefully benefit future TESOL students in several ways. Getting the view from a student who experienced the class can only help the future. I shared what helped me learn and what I will carry with me as I teach in the near future. (E-mail exchange, September 2008)

These motivations foreshadow our stories about the course design process and about involving students. As students, we (Lindsey, Jill, and Emily) wanted to participate because we recognized the potential for making the service learning field experience even better for other students. We all also believed that we could continue to learn from careful reflection about the course's design. Noteworthy here is the way our motivations for participating in the course redesign process echo the whole reason for doing service learning in the first place: to serve and to learn.

Snapshots of the Course Redesign Process

Snapshot 1: Creating Service Learning Discussion Days

Based on the redesign team's feedback, Jessie revised the course schedule to dedicate much more time to class discussion of students' service learning experiences. In previous semesters, Jessie had asked students to reflect on their service learning experiences in writing and to read and respond to their classmates' reflections, but these written conversations occurred primarily outside class. Students wanted more time for informal conversation. The following is from a coffee shop discussion with Jessie, Jill, Laurie,[2] Jenny, and Alison, May 2008:

> *Jill*: We would benefit a lot from the experiences if we talked about them in class more. I know we had the discussion board, but I was, like, it's almost whatever time and I have to post something and forgetting, because it was just like something we were supposed to get in the habit of doing. But of course, it slips your mind somehow. I feel like something's lost sometimes on the discussion board—like the flow of conversation. We [Jill and Jenny] were in the same classroom, so I would always read Jenny's stuff on the discussion board, but I feel like if we had just sat and talked more, it would be even better.
>
> *Jenny*: I agree. Unfortunately, I'm a grade-oriented person, so I would read the rubric, and it would say, "In order to get an A, you have to respond x number of times," so each week I would reply x number of times. I'd always wait for the first three posts [before I replied] so that I could get it done early and would be done for the week. So I'd be, like, that's done. Next thing.
>
> *Jessie*: So what are some of the ways that you would suggest bringing it into class?
>
> *Alison*: You could maybe do something as an intro—just to get class going—maybe a general question related to service-learning, so it's not taking up a lot of class time but so that students have a chance to talk to each other and give each other feedback.
>
> *Jill*: Or if the class meets two days a week, on the second day of the week, devote X amount of time to just discussing. "Who wants to share?"

We'll probably have some kind of topic we'll be working with that week. . . . so maybe you could facilitate it around that?

Jenny: I think it's hard though because I feel like with a lot of s-l classes, a whole lot of the content is just the s-l so all you do is come in and talk about it and that's all you have to do. With our TESOL class we had content, too, and we had to get out there and also do the service-learning hours, so it was a little bit probably harder to integrate the talking and get the content done that we needed to get done. So from that perspective, I think the discussion board would have been a good idea. It's just, for me as a learner, I'm bad with those.

Jenny: I just feel like everyone wants to talk about their placement because everyone's excited. When you have a good experience or a bad experience, everyone likes to share those experiences and find out how everyone else's placements are going. And that can be a positive, but it can also be a negative because sometimes the classroom can just shoot off in the discussion direction.

Jill: Yeah, but I get so much out of that—

Jenny [interjection]: I do too.

Jill: I don't mind staying an extra five or ten minutes if I'm actually going to walk away with something.

Based on this discussion and similar comments in the second focus group, the redesigned course dedicates one class meeting a week (out of three weekly meetings) to a discussion of the service learning field experiences. Students still write a weekly reflection, responding to a prompt that elicits connections between students' field experiences and the weekly readings, as Jill suggested, but their written posts become a starting point for 70 minutes of in-class discussion about these connections. In addition, rather than requiring x number of responses to peers' posts each week to earn an A, comments on other students' posts collectively count toward one bonus percentage point toward the final grade for the whole semester.

Snapshot 2: Negotiating the Service Learning Project

Each semester the service learning experience culminates in a project for the students' cooperating teachers and their ESL classrooms. Students negotiate possible projects that would create relevant and needed materials for the ESL classrooms, so each student's project takes a different form, but all the projects must implement what students have learned about TESOL theories and practices during the semester. The project also requires students to reflect on how their projects fulfill the ESL teachers' needs and demonstrate current TESOL theories and pedagogies. Students liked the project, but they expressed some frustrations.

The following is from the same coffee shop conversation with Jessie, Jill, Laurie, Jenny, and Alison, May 2008:

> *Jessie*: You mentioned the project. Did you feel like that brought things together for you? Was it helpful for you as a student? I know you had some challenges with it.
>
> *Laurie, Jenny, and Alison* [mixed voices]: I think it was/Yeah/I got a lot out of it.
>
> *Jenny*: I felt like with our project [Jenny and Jill's] . . . It was like I'd already written a paper and I was trying to format it for the expectations of the project requirements. We had been told that this was what she wanted for our project [a class Web site] and so it didn't exactly fit in with the specifications of the projects, so I was trying to justify it as being okay for the project. . . . I felt like that was unfortunate. Listening to some of the other projects where students got really creative— like Ben who read an entire book [recording it for a read-along package].
>
> *Jill*: We weren't even able to do anything with our interests. We had to do what she wanted us to do. And then she'd be like, "Get creative with it." But we couldn't really because it's a template. And I had to teach *them* [the cooperating ESL teachers] how to use it on top if it. . . . So, no, it didn't tie things together for me because I didn't get to use anything from the class besides putting resources for parents [on a Web site]. . . . Laurie's project was awesome. I wish I could have done something like that.
>
> *Jessie*: It sounds, though, like there needs to be more negotiation between you as a student and the cooperating teacher in selecting the project so that you have a say in it but you also get some guidance.
>
> *Laurie*: I think it's hard sometimes to have everyone to do *a* project when you don't all have the same experiences getting to know what they need. . . . It might have been easier for me to make five different *little* projects for the teachers I was working with and the individual students [rather than one project for the ESL teacher].
>
> *Alison*: I think the level of need differed a lot.

Jill: I like the fact that we did *something* for the teachers, though. I always feel bad when we go to cooperating teachers and work with them for x amount of time and then we're, like, "Okay, thanks, I got my hours, now. . . . See you later, it's been great." At least this was like a parting gift. Like, "Thank you. I can leave you with this. . . . I did something for you while I was here besides take up time." So that I really like. I would keep it [the project] for that reason.

These comments made it clear to Jessie that students needed more authority to negotiate the project with the cooperating teacher—and strategies for engaging in that negotiation. As a result, Jessie's redesigned class introduces the project earlier, prompts students to propose three projects based on a needs analysis, and then builds in time for students to discuss the project ideas in more detail with their cooperating teachers before they select one to begin drafting.

Snapshot 3: Retaining Program Profiles

In addition to dedicating more time to guided reflection on the service learning experience, Jessie also reshaped an assignment that had received mixed reviews from students. A program profile assignment asked students to complete a rhetorical analysis of an ESL program abroad or in a community other than the local municipalities. The requirements of the assignment varied. One semester the profile was a small weekly assignment with a low point value. The next year, the profile was a major assignment with a required presentation during the course's final exam time. While some students thought it was boring hearing or reading variations on a theme—rhetorical analyses examining the same features of different programs around the world—others thought the assignment provided a critical example of English language learning outside U.S. K–12 ESL classrooms.

The following is from the coffee shop conversation with Jessie, Jill, Laurie, Jenny, and Alison, May 2008:

Jill: I felt like once we'd heard a couple presentations, we weren't hearing anything new. They were so similar it quickly got boring.

The following is from a lunch conversation with Jessie, Emily, Laura, and Lindsey, May 2008:

> *Emily*: I liked the final project [the program profile] a lot. [To Laura and
> Lindsey] We picked a country and then picked a program and then
> examined the requirements to teach abroad in that program. . . . I
> liked that. It was really helpful if you're thinking of teaching abroad
> some day. With the whole class doing it, you got to hear about a lot
> of options.

A few students also noted that the assignment appealed to their classmates who were not planning a career in education but were interested in
volunteering abroad. While Jessie was aware of this alternate purpose for taking Intro to TESOL, she had tailored the course to the secondary education
English majors who were required to complete the course and reserved more
extensive discussion of other contexts for TESOL for a summer course on
teaching English abroad. The students pointed out, though, that the program profile met the needs of the diverse student audience for Intro to
TESOL and that scheduling the assignment earlier in the semester would
better engage noneducation majors in course discussions. As a result, Jessie
assigned the project in the first month of the redesigned course and used the
assignment to model the types of analyses students also should conduct for
their service learning sites. In addition, rather than spending an entire exam
period presenting the analyses, students had the opportunity during the first
20 minutes of a class period to share interesting things they had learned
about the programs they profiled. These revisions responded to the accolades
and concerns the redesign team had shared, and extended additional support
for the service learning component by letting students practice profiling
other programs before profiling their local ESL classrooms.

Additional Student-Driven Changes

Other student-driven changes in the redesigned course are reflected in Table
8.1. The fall 2006 and fall 2007 course redesigns responded to course evaluations and informal student feedback; the fall 2008 course redesign also
reflected feedback from students involved in the redesign project, and six
student participants commented on an early draft of the syllabus for the
semester.

As Table 8.1 reflects, the fall 2008 redesign focused more attention on
the service learning portion of the course, with weekly in-class discussions
about the service learning experience and a public wiki to showcase service

TABLE 8.1
Course Features Redesigned Based on Student Feedback

Fall 2006	Fall 2007	Fall 2008
Two 100-minute classes/week	Three 70-minute classes/week	Three 70-minute classes/week
Periodic written reflections about service learning	Weekly reflections with required responses	Weekly reflections with in-class discussion
Weekly homework, sometimes related to service learning	Weekly homework, sometimes related to service learning	
One weekly homework conducting a program profile of an ESL program abroad in November	Final paper and presentation in December conducting a rhetorical analysis of an ESL program abroad	Paper conducting a rhetorical analysis of an ESL program abroad, drafted and revised in September
Eight weeks to work on service learning project	Nine weeks to work on service learning project, with project proposal	Nine weeks to work on service learning project, with extended proposal process
Additional classwide service learning project		Service learning projects posted on public wiki
Graduate-level language teaching textbook	Two TESOL texts for preservice and in-service teachers; one second language acquisition text	Two TESOL texts for preservice and in-service teachers
Three exams	Two exams	Two comprehensive exams
Language policy paper	Language policy paper	Language policy paper

learning projects where students and cooperating teachers could access them in the future. While students still had required readings for most class sessions and weekly written reflections, Jessie eliminated other weekly homework assignments and replaced them with in-class activities. This revision enabled students to spend more of their out-of-class time focused on the service learning experience and related guided reflections.

Snapshots of Student Voices in Course Redesign

Involving students in redesigning a course benefits the future students and the students and faculty participating in the redesign project. As Jill and Emily's comments from our September e-mail exchange (p. 126) suggest, student voices are invaluable for redesigning courses because the students have lived the course experience and can provide strong rationales for retaining or changing features of the course.

The suggestions we students gave Jessie for the TESOL class were nearly unanimous. Collectively, we also were able to validate individual members' suggestions because we understand how these suggestions would work for our diverse learning styles. Therefore, we believe the input will be very beneficial for future students of the course. Since Jessie can tell future students that we participated in redesigning the course, we believe future students might be more inclined to accept the course requirements, including the service learning component. We already have learned that the fall 2008 students consider the service learning discussions helpful for understanding why they are volunteering in ESL classrooms and for connecting the service learning experiences to the course content. One fall 2008 student even reported:

> Friday [service learning] discussions are my favorite part of the class. Fridays are the day you don't want to miss because you know it will be the most beneficial to you. Talking about what is going on at our service learning sites and getting feedback from each other as well as the professor has been really helpful in making connections to what we have learned during other class periods, from the readings, and from other experiences. (Anonymous, personal communication, December 4, 2008)

Responses like this one have demonstrated that the incorporation and consideration of our concerns has helped to create a more learner-friendly curriculum. Talking about the service learning experiences as a group facilitates valuable oral reflections, allowing students to voice questions or talk through disconnects between their service learning experiences and the course materials. While Jessie provides a weekly topic to focus the discussions on, students have the leeway to bring up questions and issues they are grappling with as they reflect on their volunteer time in the ESL classes. Therefore, the Friday discussions focus on learners' needs as they process new material.

Furthermore, we—Emily, Lindsey, and Jill—were able to approach the redesign as students and as teachers because we had taken the course, and because as teacher licensure candidates we are aware of how much work designing a simple lesson plan can be. As students in the School of Education, we had the advantage of fulfilling student and teacher roles, and we benefited from reflecting on and participating in the course redesign. We tried to give Jessie recommendations that were not only honest but also practical.

Yet those benefits are paired with challenges that course redesign team members should plan ahead for. Faculty and students are very busy, so getting everyone together can be a significant challenge. Jessie invited a diverse group of students to participate, with representatives of both genders from two semesters and from various stages in their major course of study. While this range of variables likely led to a richer set of student input, it proved impossible to gather everyone at one time. As a result, she met with two subgroups at separate times. Finding time for everyone to meet is a notable challenge, so anticipating that the process will take twice as long as hoped makes the time component less stressful.

We learned that time could work against us in other ways too. For the participants who had taken TESOL nearly a year and a half before participating in the redesign project, it was difficult at times to remember specifics about pacing and the course structure. Nevertheless, we could recall the most significant aspects of our original courses: our service learning field experiences and our service learning projects. Our clear recollections of these projects reiterated the importance for connecting the field's scholarship to practices in ESL classrooms.

In addition to the challenge of finding the right time to meet, including student voices presented us with other challenges as well. Most notably, we had to consider how to negotiate shifting power dynamics.

Snapshot 4: Considering Power Dynamics

The most difficult part of the redesign project was bridging the gap between student and teacher. Although Jessie was unlikely to have the same students in future classes unless they pursued undergraduate research projects or independent study with her, she remained Lindsey, Emily, and Jill's professor in a teacher licensure program that emphasizes professionalism and calls on students to "interact with colleagues, students, families and others in the community in an ethical and respectful manner" (Elon University, School of Education, n.d.). Even as faculty like Jessie try to recognize students' expertise and their future roles as colleagues, the university requirement for faculty to complete disposition forms about students' professionalism may reinforce the unequal power dynamics between students and teachers.[3] The following discussion exemplifies this paradox:

> *Emily*: I have never told a teacher my suggestions on his/her class, and I didn't want to cross the line. However, it was beneficial for me to review the class and understand the strengths and weaknesses of how a classroom is run. I see the difficulty in getting students totally involved in the classroom and establishing what works and doesn't through a teacher's perspective.
>
> *Jill*: I feel like I have learned how to work collaboratively through the example set by my professor and my peers. We were able to sit around and speak openly, informally, and intellectually about TESOL and how it should be taught. I enjoyed this experience tremendously. (E-mail exchange, September 2008)

Jessie did too. Because the students were willing to push the traditional roles shaped by student/teacher boundaries, she gained invaluable insight into how the service learning project informed students' TESOL experiences. Fortunately, students benefited from the course redesign experience too.

Snapshot 5: Continuing Our TESOL Education

While future students clearly profit from the course redesign process, it also extended the learning process for the former TESOL students. All of us were able to reflect on our service learning experiences and how we had connected the TESOL course content to subsequent course work and field experiences.

Emily: Learning through experience (i.e., talking about our service learning) in schools helped me realize what a teacher does. Showing how the information we learn in the classroom connects to what we can do in our future jobs makes it that much more useful to us students.

Lindsey: The pedagogy behind working with English Language Learners is certainly more widely applicable to other fields. After TESOL, I was able to pair that knowledge with teaching composition and working with students who have learning disabilities and other special needs.

Jillian: There were primarily two benefits I found in participating in the redesign of the course: I was able to feel like I was a part of something that would have a positive effect on the way future students of TESOL viewed the course and I was able to understand how difficult, and yet rewarding, creating a curriculum could be. (E-mail exchange, September 2008)

Conclusion

Given the rewards of redesigning a course by including student voices, we highly recommend this process to other educators. Therefore, the first strategy we suggest to professors who are interested or intrigued by the idea of incorporating students' opinions in a course redesign is simple: *Do it*!

Second, we suggest that the professor prepare pointed questions for group meetings but not be afraid of going slightly off topic; some of our best ideas came from the flow of conversation. We learned that simply talking together about our views on the course helped us reconceptualize it. However, without a starting point, students may be slightly intimidated and unsure of where to start. And for students, we say that honesty is the best policy; there's no sense in offering your opinion if you are going to be timid. Your professor will value your opinion, and your participation can help future students and your own development as a learner and as a future professional.

Third, participants also should consider the logistics of the course redesign process. We found it worked best to coordinate our meetings with meals. Faculty members and undergraduate students are all busy, but they have to eat just like everyone else, so combining our meetings with meals accomplished two important tasks. Fourth, we also recommend meeting in multiple small groups. If all eight of us had met at once, the process easily could be intimidating. With two smaller groups we all felt like we could contribute; rather than bandwagon responses, we could offer more individual reactions. In addition, Jessie benefited from being able to verify ideas by running them past two groups.

Finally, we also profited from extending our face-to-face conversations via e-mail discussions. E-mail gave us more time to think about what we were writing and helped us work around time constraints created by our busy schedules. In the future we might try using Google Docs, or a similar collaborative writing tool, to further enhance our asynchronous contributions.

Overall, we want to reiterate the value to the faculty member, to future students, and to redesign participants of including student voices in course redesigns. All parties benefit, which is why Jessie will continue the process in future semesters. And if the whole point of using service learning is to serve community while serving learning—everyone's learning—it seems especially useful to include students in redesigning service learning courses.

Notes

1. Although the field of TESOL uses a variety of terms to specify unique contexts for English learning and instruction, we use ESL as an umbrella term throughout this chapter.

2. Four of our course design collaborators opted not to participate in writing about our experience. We appreciate their contributions to the redesign process and their consent to let us include their voices in our chapter through transcriptions of our earlier conversations.

3. At Elon teacher licensure candidates are assessed (and self-assess) using disposition forms several times during their undergraduate careers. The School of Education uses these forms to help evaluate students' professionalism and engagement as future teachers. A poor assessment on a disposition form could jeopardize a student's future in the education program. The forms risk suggesting to faculty-student partners that the faculty member is always in an evaluative role rather than part of a collaborative partnership.

References

Elon University, School of Education. (n.d.). *Teacher education mission*. Retrieved October 1, 2008, from http://www.elon.edu/e-web/academics/education/teachered/mission.xhtml

Kapper, J. M., Clapp, L., & Lefferts, C. (2007). TESOL in context: Student perspectives on service-learning. In A. Wurr & J. Hellebrandt (Eds.), *Learning the language of global citizenship: Service-learning in applied linguistics* (pp. 141–163). Bolton: Anker.

9

ENGAGING STUDENTS AS SCHOLARS OF TEACHING AND LEARNING

The Role of Ownership

*Ellen E. Gutman, Erin M. Sergison,
Chelsea J. Martin, and Jeffrey L. Bernstein*

All too often, teaching happens in isolation (Shulman 1993).[1] Too much good work in the classroom disappears because teaching rarely produces artifacts to represent results, such as scholarly research produces articles and books. Additionally, teaching suffers because we do not talk about it enough. Dialogue about teaching is difficult since, as Bass (1999) suggests, teaching is not as readily "problematized" as research. Problems in traditional research initiate a germinative process, creating the opportunity for scholars to interact and collaborate; problems in teaching rarely generate discussion, as those who have a problem in their teaching probably prefer to minimize that fact rather than use it as a conversation starter. The solution, Shulman (2004) suggests, is to make teaching community property by encouraging discussion about teaching, formally (in books and journals) and informally (at the proverbial water cooler). We join our colleagues in this volume in suggesting that these conversations are particularly valuable when we hold them with students; this dialogue creates a culture that fosters collaboration and helps to facilitate the productive problematizing of teaching.

This chapter describes a collaborative teaching project that emerged over 3 years in an American government class at Eastern Michigan University

(EMU). Professor Bernstein worked on this project with co-authors Gutman, Sergison, and Martin when they were undergraduates at EMU. These 3, along with 14 other students, served as simulation facilitators, research assistants, and seminar participants between 2005 and 2008. Our chapter describes that partnership, traces its results, and discusses determinants of success. Our focus here is on the work Bernstein did with the simulation facilitators. For this chapter, Bernstein's American government class provides the background and context for our inquiry. We describe that background and context, but we do not explore the learning that took place among these students; interested readers may consult Bernstein (2008) for evidence of learning on the part of the American government students.

To preview our findings, we observed that the key factor determining the success of the model appears to be the degree of *ownership* of the project the facilitators had. When the students perceived themselves to be full partners in the project, the experience worked better. When they saw themselves as less than full partners, the experience still provided benefits but did not have the same impact as when the ownership level was higher. We conclude by discussing the implications of our findings.

Collaborative Work in the American Government Class

The collaborative inquiry project described here emerged from Bernstein's year as a Carnegie scholar, which led him to reconsider the introductory American government course he had been teaching. The course had used large-scale American government simulations in which students played members of Congress, members of the presidential administration, lobbyists, and journalists. The simulation was fun to do and created powerful learning opportunities (see Bernstein & Meizlish, 2003, for more on the simulation's effect on the students).

Despite the simulation's successes, Bernstein decided it needed to be improved. Students were mastering the rules of the game but often failed to make connections between the simulation and real-world American politics. Focusing on the *politics* of passing legislation emphasizes important lessons but often at the expense of the *policy* aspects of the game. Students might learn how to trade votes and lobby to pass Social Security reform, but their knowledge of Social Security policy was limited. Furthermore, the emphasis on the political aspects risked exposing students to that part of democracy that is often found most distasteful (Hibbing & Theiss-Morse, 1995); unwittingly, in creating this simulation Bernstein risked magnifying the cynicism and disengagement he worked to overcome.

In redesigning the simulations, Bernstein was guided by the idea of civic competence (Lupia, 2006). This course would likely be the only university-level political science course taken by 90% of his students; as such, he wanted to ensure they would emerge as civically competent citizens with the skills needed to participate in politics when or if they were motivated to do so.[2] Students must be able to integrate what they learn in class with what happens in the real world, allowing them to follow the news, form nuanced opinions about thorny issues, and discuss politics with others. Helping them gain these competencies required a fundamental redesign of the course (Bernstein, 2008).

Following Wiggins and McTighe's (1998) backward design model, wherein instructors determine the goals of their class and then work backward to help the course achieve the goals, Bernstein considered what would be required for cultivating his students' civic competence. He defined a civically competent student as one who could

- manage political information—making sense of a vast and complex array of political information to reach intelligent judgments on political issues;
- master the interpersonal aspects of politics—working with allies to achieve collective action while maintaining civility when working in opposition to others;
- realize the link between rules and outcomes—understanding how the rules in a political system drive results, knowing how to try adjusting the rules to yield a desired outcome.

He designed the new simulations with these end goals in mind.

He began to design what the simulations might look like when implemented in the classroom.[3] The new design of the simulations focused on substantive political issues.[4] The students in the course were divided into smaller groups and would engage in each simulation for 1 week.[5] Before the simulation, students would read 8 to 10 short articles (one to two pages each) on that issue. The articles represented the collective information available on that issue; they included news articles, opinion pieces, blogs, political speeches, and other sources from a wide array of viewpoints. Students read the articles and wrote a paper expressing their view on the issue, using the articles to defend their position and raise or rebut opinions on the other side.

During the simulation, the students worked to make policy on the issue. Students received a one-page summary sheet of policy in that area (the status quo).[6] They began the simulation with two rounds of *think-pair-share* in which students discussed their views with classmates. Next they wrote proposals aimed at changing aspects of the status quo, circulating through the room as they were writing to seek the advice and support of classmates. Proposals required three signatures to be considered in debate; students were encouraged to canvass the room as much as possible to build support for their ideas.

Proposal writing took place on days 1 and 2.[7] On day 3, students engaged in debate on the proposals. The day began with a Rules Committee meeting to determine which of the accumulated proposals would be considered for debate, in what order, and under what rules (e.g., majority or two-thirds vote to pass a proposal, voting by secret ballot or show of hands). Members of the Rules Committee were sometimes appointed by the simulation facilitator, other times they were elected by the class. After the Rules Committee met, discussion and voting on the proposals took place. Debriefing followed the simulations when students returned to the full class.

Addressing a Problem, Seeking an Answer

As attractive as the course design seemed, it presented a logistical problem. The need for smaller groups was clear; groups of 70 or 100 would be too large for effective participatory learning to occur because students would too easily be able to avoid participating in class discussions. Multiple groups, however, might require four simulations to occur simultaneously. One instructor would not be able to cover four classes at one time, so Bernstein decided to involve undergraduate students as simulation facilitators and ultimately as collaborators. He offered independent study credit to strong students who were interested in studying political science, civic engagement, and teaching and learning for their participation in the project.[8] In the 1st year, students all came from the university's Honors College; in the 2nd year, all but one was in the Honors College. By year 3, half of the six were not honors students; all students, however, had strong GPAs and a track record of academic achievement.

The decision to use strong students was intentional. These students would be teaching their fellow students while facilitating the simulations. Bernstein needed to be sure they were capable of doing this well. These students needed the ability to think on their feet when presented with unanticipated arguments, the capacity for tolerating and embracing disagreement among the students, and the ability to tackle complicated material even though they were initially not interested. The success of nonhonors students in the 3rd year suggests this experience need not be offered only to honors students; our experience, however, suggests the typical undergraduate is probably not equipped with the level of expertise required to be a simulation facilitator.

Bernstein came to see collaborative inquiry as a solution to problems he had considered but not addressed. First was how to provide challenging learning experiences for strong students at a heterogeneous institution. In EMU's upper-level classes, instructors struggle to challenge the strongest students for fear of losing the weaker students. Consequently, strong students realize they can survive with minimal effort; their natural abilities would suffice. Bernstein sought a way to challenge top students to do their best work without hurting other students.

Second, Bernstein had begun to think more about epistemology. He wanted to design courses that would focus on the boundaries of what we know and do not know about a topic, and on how we create knowledge in the discipline. This project offered an opportunity to work with top-notch students in collaborative inquiry that focused on what we do and do not know about learning in political science; the facilitators were not mere consumers of knowledge but were instead directly involved in creating knowledge on this topic (through significant term papers). It represented a more authentic way for students to learn their discipline.[9]

In addition, facilitators believe this project provided them with other benefits. First, these students worked closely with a faculty member, something relatively few students do while in college, and this experience has been shown to help students make the most of their college experience (Light, 2001). Breaking down walls between faculty and students helped them develop a relationship not only with Bernstein but also with other professors.

Moreover, facilitators report that running the simulations taught them skills such as leadership and facilitation. Bernstein had not explicitly aimed for that, nor had he particularly expected it to occur. The student co-authors of this chapter suggested exploring these skills based upon their own experiences, leading us to include a related question when we interviewed the former facilitators.[10] When asked if the experience of facilitating the simulations had affected the way they take leadership roles, students responded with answers such as

- "In a way. I tend to take a facilitation approach rather than a dominating approach. In Circle K, I am the president, but I look at myself as more a facilitator. I'm not sure I was any different from this at the start, but this project has given me more confidence in my ability to lead this way."
- "Yes, with ROTC. I use a lot of the stuff I learned from the simulations for that."
- "I was site director for my summer camp last year. I was in charge, and there were 8 counselors and fifteen kids. The experience did not directly affect how I led the group. I guess it did have an effect on leading the counselors, and leading staff members. . . . Maybe more confidence in my ability."

Thus, the experience benefited the students in ways beyond what had originally been envisioned.

Student Roles—Building Collaborative Inquiry

In planning this project, the scope of the collaboration expanded. It began with the students working as teaching assistants (simulation facilitators) for the professor. They had no other formal responsibilities in the class but were expected to attend the first few days (to get a sense of Bernstein's approach to the class) and on days he was introducing and debriefing the simulations. Originally the students were laborers first and collaborators second.[11]

True collaboration began to occur in the evolution of the project and the expansion of facilitators' roles. The facilitators worked as research assistants on Bernstein's scholarship of teaching and learning investigation. For example, Bernstein was analyzing and coding student essays, looking for evidence of increased skill working with political information—a daunting task for one researcher but feasible when the facilitators assisted. The students gained firsthand experience in the research process and learned how knowledge is created in political science and in teaching and learning.

A second expansion of the facilitators' role was the opportunity to participate in a seminar experience. The seminar met most weeks. Students did reading on political engagement (e.g., Dionne, 1991), political knowledge (Delli Carpini & Keeter, 1996), and social capital (Putnam, 2000). This reading provided background on citizenship goals; understanding students' lack of political engagement, knowledge, and social capital helped facilitators understand how to teach students less politically engaged than themselves. The students learned techniques for facilitating simulations, including dealing with explosive issues in classroom discussion. They also learned not only about the political issues in question but also about how to *teach about* these issues—what Shulman (1987) termed *pedagogical content knowledge*. Students were expected to conduct their own independent research on student learning in the class as part of the seminar experience.

Collaborative inquiry presented challenges, opportunities, pitfalls, and uncertainties, often at the same time. Bernstein quickly realized the benefits from having a group of collaborators who would read the same things he was reading, think about the same issues he was puzzling over, and experience the classroom environment he observed. In so doing, seminar students could become true collaborators in his inquiry. In the following sections, we explore degrees of success in the project.

Ownership and Collaborative Inquiry

We begin our analysis by emphasizing that *ownership* is a linchpin for collaboration. By ownership we mean a sense on the part of the facilitators that the experience was shared between them and the professor, where all partners guided the project's direction. All involved in the project, including interview respondents and co-authors, expressed a sense of shared responsibility for its success and a sense that they were partners in helping to ensure that success. This feeling of ownership intensified as facilitators' ideas were put into practice to improve the simulations. Facilitators noted:

- "Dr. Bernstein was very open to our perceptions of how things were working like why things were different in the winter semester than they were in the fall semester. He definitely took what we said into consideration and asked for our input. We worked through a lot of the problems of the simulations together."
- "With simulations [Bernstein] gave us goals and we were able to carry it out in our own way so long as we followed the basic ideas. The way we interacted [with simulation participants] was up to us; we . . . had a strong involvement in the whole process."
- "The facilitators as a group shaped the topics. They all ran simulations a little differently."

Most of the facilitators agreed that their opinions and ideas changed how the simulations were conducted. The students believed they were more than assistants who carry out the professor's design. Instead, they were collaborators with Bernstein, helping him develop the details of the project by suggesting new ideas to improve the students' learning experience.

Ownership is clearly critical for the project's success; why this is the case is a more difficult question. Nathan's (2005) book about an anthropology professor doing fieldwork as a 1st-year college student may shed light on this process. Nathan finds that undergraduate students perceive themselves as having little agency over the academic components of their college careers. Whereas they experience greater freedom in virtually all other aspects of their lives, academic *classes* are typically run by a professor who chooses the readings, assessment methods, and how the classes are run.[12] Students are often passive recipients of the professor's knowledge rather than partners in the teaching and learning process. In other aspects of their life, undergraduates are treated as adults with the agency to make decisions that affect them; in the classroom, Nathan suggests students may feel somewhat alienated.[13] Giving facilitators greater control of their educational experience ought to translate into greater engagement, and more significant learning.

As a corollary to ownership, we propose that the most successful iterations of the seminar gave the facilitators a project that was distinctively theirs. The facilitators in the first and third cohorts did a group, public presentation in a campuswide event about their experience and about student learning in the political science course. This shared experience helped connect the students to each other interpersonally and made them even more invested in the project. Preparing for these presentations was intense; the instructor's physical presence as the students worked helped narrow the gap between faculty and student. Rather than seeing the professor as an external force imposing instructions on his students, the students were in control as they developed the presentations (Bernstein offered guidance when needed). Facilitators described to us in great detail the confidence they gained working through the difficulties and celebrating the successes of these public presentations.

In retrospect, we see that the extent of ownership varied from year to year. Some of the participants developed a sense of ownership in the project while others did not; this individual-level variation is commonplace whenever we study student behavior and attitudes. More interesting is that some *cohorts* of facilitators developed a greater sense of ownership than did others. The first cohort developed a higher sense of ownership than did the next two, and the third cohort showed more ownership than the second. In the next section, we briefly detail the experiences of these cohorts; we follow this with some analysis to explain the puzzle of ownership.

A Tale of Three Experiences: Ownership and the Three Seminar Groups

The First Simulation—Starting From Scratch, Together

The decision to use this teaching model was made in July 2005. The semester would begin in 7 weeks; most students had completed their course schedules for the upcoming term. To populate the seminar, Bernstein e-mailed students in the Honors College and upper-level political science students. The students who responded included three who had taken a nontraditional class with Bernstein and were willing to take this leap of faith.[14] Two additional students learned about the course and enrolled (one left the project after the first semester for personal reasons).

In this iteration of the seminar, Bernstein walked in with no syllabus, just a sheet of paper that explained what the class would be discussing that week and what to read for next week. The seminar progressed similarly, each week preparing for the next and not much more. On the 1st day Bernstein explained that he did not provide a syllabus because he did not know exactly what the class would be doing for the rest of the semester; he had ideas for things to read but chose to follow students' interests and the evolving project in determining the seminar's direction. If a student had an idea about what the seminar participants should be discussing, Bernstein was open to suggestions. Our goal was to make it *our* seminar and not *his* seminar.

Bernstein first noticed the use of "our project" language in December as he was reviewing facilitators' proposals for their research projects. Rather than referring to "the project" or "Bernstein's project," they all referred to our project and things "we" should do. Bernstein felt intense gratification; he realized his students were becoming invested in the project, and sink or swim, they felt responsible for its success.

In this 1st year only, facilitators worked alone in their simulations; in later cohorts, students facilitated simulation in teams of two, allowing for more interaction with each student in the class. While this change was undoubtedly the right decision, working alone did create greater accountability for the facilitators; while Bernstein moved between rooms to assist in each simulation, the facilitators were largely responsible for what happened in their rooms. This additional responsibility undoubtedly led to increased engagement in the project.

Another aspect of their engagement was this group's presentation on the project during EMU's Undergraduate Research Symposium in March 2006. Preparing for the presentation was intense; the facilitators worked late nights and early mornings together to create a successful presentation. The presentation focused on the collaborative inquiry model as well as on the government students' learning within the simulations. In presenting their work, they answered challenging questions from the audience, leading them to defend the project as their own work rather than as a course assignment they had invested little in. Most importantly, it was *their* presentation—Bernstein introduced them and then watched them shine.

The Second Simulation—A Little Knowledge Is a Dangerous Thing

In the later iterations of the seminar, Bernstein had a clearer idea of what should happen. In keeping with his detail-oriented nature and his desire to let students know what to expect, he created a structured syllabus and course outline—the 2nd year's syllabus was 10 pages long and included detailed reading assignments for each seminar meeting. While this syllabus was not set in stone—it emphasized in numerous places that it was tentative and could be changed to accommodate evolving interests—it did not allow the same level of malleability the 1st year had. In retrospect, the details of this syllabus likely hindered the development of ownership and may have led students to feel like participants in their professor's project, not part of a collaborative project in which the structure developed jointly.

To be sure, facilitators did continue to play a critical role in the project. But the tone felt different, as the interviews reveal. For example, one student noted, "It was [Bernstein's] project and [he] helped to guide us to the end results, but we had group decisions on aspects of it—timing, how many proposals, how we were going to vote." This facilitator notes they did have input in how the project unfolded; these were not minor decisions that they helped make. But the overall tone was different: this was Bernstein's project, and not *their* project.

A related point concerns the students' interpersonal bonding. The first group seemed to gel much better than the second group; one student in the second group noted, "I'm not sure the facilitators really bonded with one another—not sure why this was the case." One explanation may be that the first group, including the instructor, was facing an unknown and unfamiliar challenge, leading them to bond with each other. The second group confronted similar challenges but perhaps with a little less urgency, given that the instructor seemed to have more answers by the time they came together. The instructor's knowledge may have led to a smoother seminar but not without a cost.

One student suggests that the demographics of the group were another reason the second group did not bond as well: "The hardest part was that myself and [another student] were the only seniors and . . . the other ones were a lot younger. There was kind of an age gap." While this age difference may explain some of the issues, there was also an age gap in the other groups, both of which bonded more tightly. One other factor is that this group did not make a presentation on the project to any larger audience. These presentations were critical as unifying tools to the first and third groups; their absence this year may be significant in explaining why this group felt less ownership. In reflection, Bernstein concluded that he had swung the pendulum too far, and that students did not have sufficient ownership in this seminar.

The Third Simulation–Restoring Some Ownership

The third iteration of the simulation sought to capture some of the magic of the first one. The possibilities for doing this were limited because the newness of the first iteration could not be repeated; still, aware that the previous group had not attained as much ownership, Bernstein tried to encourage it more with the facilitators. It appears this did happen. For example, one student, when asked if she felt that her ideas ever changed what happened in the simulations, laughingly exclaimed, "We shaped them; we made him change them all the time!" Students worked together on enhancing collaborative inquiry; one noted, "The collaborative environment helps all of us, because if something isn't working we can ask the other two groups to help us out with the method to see what's working or not, to get a sense of what to do next time." These facilitators express a feeling we share: Collaboration made the class succeed. The seminar became a time for interaction where the students supported each other through difficulties and challenged each other to think creatively about ways to approach future simulations.

The key bonding moment for this group was its presentation at EMU's Symposium on Democracy in Our Wiki World. During the winter semester, facilitators worked with Bernstein to outline the presentation (focusing on how the simulations helped to make students more capable of confronting vast amounts of political information). Once the outline was created and the tasks divided, each student developed slides about his or her speaking points; the group then worked together to complete the presentation. This involved numerous meetings during the days leading up to the event, and a late-night meeting that extended almost until midnight the night before the presentation.

The symposium presentation used Bernstein's data (content analysis of student essays that the facilitators had helped to code) to make empirical arguments about the simulations' effects on information literacy. The facilitators, however, molded their theoretical ideas and the data into a presentation that needed to be their own. While creating the presentation, they found overlaps in their own ideas about the project; they debated with each other and found they had developed an attachment to the research. They started by referring to the presentation as "our presentation" (Bernstein introduced them and presented one concluding slide); by the end, they referred to the data as "our data" and had full ownership of the presentation. This experience brought the group closer and took their research and engagement to a new level. As one student told us, the experience was "empowering" for these students.

Discussion

By any measure, the collaborative inquiry model used in the Political Science 112 course was a success. Over 3 years, 17 students worked with Bernstein as simulation facilitators, research assistants, seminar participants, and, in 2 of the 3 years, co-presenters at university-wide symposia. Minimally, this collaboration provided a more interactive and engaging academic experience than most students get. By the end of the project, all facilitators interviewed expressed appreciation for having had this opportunity. Their work made possible significant innovation in Bernstein's American government class; more than being assistants, however, these students became collaborators.

We have learned that the more we can give students *ownership*, the more we can leverage the value of their experience. The opportunity to develop a new project is a significant source of ownership. When Bernstein concluded seminar meetings the 1st year by asking, "What do you want to read for next week?" the facilitators knew they were partners in the project, not passive recipients of someone else's knowledge. In the moment when Bernstein told the facilitators, "*You* will be doing the presentation at the symposium; I'll be on the side thinking good thoughts for you," the facilitators knew they owned that part of the experience. And when Bernstein solicited ideas from the facilitators on how to solve problems in the simulations, *and listened to them*, the facilitators knew they were stakeholders and not hired help.

These examples should serve as a guideline to faculty who are attempting to design effective collaborative inquiry experiences with their students. This principle is important: If our colleagues in the academy want to take the step into collaborative inquiry, we hope our examples (positive and less positive) will guide them. However, perhaps the largest lesson of this chapter involves exploring *why* ownership matters. Our experiences suggest that students crave this sense of ownership and involvement in their education. While providing collaborative inquiry opportunities, such as the facilitators had here, is not feasible for more than a handful of students, it is worth all our attention to consider how we can help more students take ownership of their education. Clearly it requires a redefinition of the faculty role, perhaps to do less and a redefinition of the student role to do more. Such a shift will not be easy; however, we believe that effectively educating our students requires that we find ways to make them full partners in, rather than passive recipients of, their education.

Notes

1. Thanks to the Carnegie Foundation for providing a hospitable environment for Bernstein's work, and to Pat Hutchings, Rebecca Nowacek, Carmen Werder, and Megan Otis for their many helpful comments. Our critical friends (Kathleen McKinney, Betsy Decyk, and their colleagues) provided useful advice that has improved this chapter. The College of Arts and Sciences and the Honors College at Eastern Michigan University funded conference travel for the student coauthors, which proved invaluable in helping create ownership of the project. Finally, we would like to thank the simulation facilitators who shared their insights on this project with us.

2. During the first 2 years of this project, the introductory American government course was required for *all* EMU students as part of the university's general education program; most of them would not be enrolling in subsequent political science courses. Effective September 2007, that requirement was removed for new students entering the university; the course is now part of a menu of social science courses from which students select two. Even in 2007–08 most students were still governed by the old requirements; thus, the overwhelming majority of students did not take the class of their own volition.

3. As will become clear from the description of the simulations, using them would be impossible without classroom assistance. Thus, the students' role was defined *after* the basic design was put in place. While not present in the original planning and design, student voicse were heard clearly in the implementation and redesign.

4. Original issues included affirmative action, eminent domain, school prayer, and the war on terror. Subsequently, eminent domain was dropped; the class focused on three issues. During the winter 2008 semester, affirmative action and the war on terror were dropped, and capital punishment was added.

5. Class typically met for 50 minutes, 3 days a week. In the fall 2007 term, class met twice a week for 75 minutes. Fall term enrollment typically was 100 students in four groups; winter term enrollment was closer to 70 students in three groups.

6. In the provision of the status quo sheet, the facilitators were directly involved in the redesign of the simulations. Originally students were asked to design policy on the issue without the benefit of such a sheet. The facilitators first suggested that such a sheet would be helpful, after the first two simulations of the fall 2005 semester. They also helped draft the status quo sheets for each of the simulation issues.

7. The schedule was adjusted slightly when the simulation unfolded over two 75-minute class sessions.

8. Independent study is a useful idea for faculty without the resources to pay students for this work.

9. We are fortunate there is a link between studying political science and studying teaching and learning in political science; the field of political socialization focuses on the processes by which political information is learned. There is less of a divide between these two areas than in other disciplines.

10. In addition to using our own autobiographical reflections, we draw on interviews we conducted with 10 of the 14 students who served as facilitators between 2005 and 2006 and 2007 and 2008 (this does not include the three facilitators who are coauthors). Gutman and Sergison were facilitators the 1st year of this project in 2005–06, while Martin was a facilitator during 2007–08. One of the remaining two facilitators was interviewed from the first group, five of the seven facilitators were interviewed from the second group, and four of the remaining five facilitators from the third group were interviewed. Interviews were semistructured conversations about the experience, each lasting 25 to 30 minutes. Interviewers took notes and transcribed them immediately thereafter. Interviews took place with approval from the EMU Human Subjects Review Committee.

11. It was not until after the 1st year that the idea formed for students to collaborate on scholarly writing based on the experience. Bernstein, Gutman, and Sergison presented this work at the International Society for the Scholarship of Teaching and Learning Conference in 2006; they were joined by Martin on a presentation at Western Washington University's Festival of Scholarship in 2008. This chapter builds upon work presented at those meetings.

12. We distinguish between *classes*, where students typically have less control over their learning experience, and their overall *program*, where students have greater opportunity to develop their own experience (by choosing majors and minors, and even which classes to take). This greater freedom is somewhat limited by general education requirements that often force students (for good reason) to take classes they would prefer not to take.

13. Nathan's (2005) conversations with students suggest that many look at their classes as a necessary, albeit minimally valued, requirement if they wish to engage in the college experience.

14. This honors seminar in political science research methods was an applied class where students did a research report for the honors program on how to increase diversity in the program. Students became accustomed to Bernstein's enjoyment of teaching and learning in an applied setting, or as he calls it, "teaching without a net." These students also bonded interpersonally, contributing to the success of the first seminar.

References

Bass, R. (1999). The scholarship of teaching: What's the problem? *Inventio, 1*(1), 1–10.

Bernstein, J. L. (2008). Cultivating civic competence: Simulations and skill-building in an introductory government class. *Journal of Political Science Education, 4*(1), 1–20.

Bernstein, J. L., & Meizlish, D. S. (2003). Becoming Congress: A longitudinal study of the civic engagement implications of a classroom simulation. *Simulation & Gaming, 34*(2), 198–219.

Delli Carpini, M. X., & Keeter, S. (1996). *What Americans know about politics and why it matters*. New Haven, CT: Yale University Press.

Dionne, E. J. (1991). *Why Americans hate politics*. New York: Simon & Schuster.

Hibbing, J. R., & Theiss-Morse, E. (1995). *Congress as public enemy: Public attitudes toward American political institutions*. New York: Cambridge University Press.

Light, R. J. (2001). *Making the most of college*. Cambridge, MA: Harvard University Press.

Lupia, A. (2006). How elitism undermines the study of voter competence. *Critical Review, 18*(1), 217–232.

Nathan, R. N. (2005). *My freshman year: What a professor learned by becoming a student*. New York: Cornell University Press.

Putnam, R. D. (2000). *Bowling alone: The collapse and revival of American community*. New York: Simon & Schuster.

Shulman, L. S. (1987). Knowledge and teaching: Foundations of the new reform. *Harvard Educational Review, 36*, 1–22.

Shulman, L. S. (1993). Teaching as community property: Putting an end to pedagogical solitude. *Change, 6*, 6–7.

Shulman, L. S. (2004). *Teaching as community property: Essays on higher education*. San Francisco: Jossey-Bass.

Wiggins, G., & McTighe, J. (1998). *Understanding by design*. Alexandria, VA: Association for Supervision and Curriculum Development.

10

STUDENT VOICES THROUGH RESEARCHING AND PROMOTING LEARNER AUTONOMY

Michael D. Sublett, Jeffrey A. Walsh,
Kathleen McKinney, and Denise Faigao

I n this chapter we offer information and examples from an internal scholarship of teaching and learning (SoTL) small-grant program; one of its functions is to offer a way to hear student voices in teaching, learning, and SoTL.[1] We begin by briefly summarizing the history and current status of the grant program and the place of student voices and learner autonomy in that program. Next, we present an overview of four of the projects including findings on learner autonomy and the roles of students. The third section of the chapter lays out the themes or patterns that emerged from interviews with faculty and student members of the small-grant research teams about learner autonomy and student voices. Finally, we conclude with some advice for others interested in promoting learner autonomy and inviting students into SoTL as research collaborators.

A Brief History of the Illinois State University SoTL Grant Program

At Illinois State University, as in many institutions of higher education, we offer small grants for conducting SoTL research (McKinney, 2008). Our

SoTL grant program began in the late 1990s and was originally very general in terms of grant topics and eligibility requirements. Over time the program developed, and changes in the guidelines have been used to obtain submissions that fit institutional priorities in our SoTL work. These priorities have included obtaining student voices in SoTL and promoting learner autonomy.

We began these changes in the grant program by first moving from a broad view of SoTL that included SoTL research, scholarly teaching, and teaching improvement or techniques to a more refined view of SoTL as "the systematic study/reflection of teaching and learning made public" (Illinois State University, 2009b). Members of the university community adopted this formal definition in 1998. We continue to support scholarly teaching and teaching improvement projects where some form of data, broadly defined, is not obtained and/or not made public with other funds. Second, we made the decision to move from individual grants to small team grants, and depending on the year and our objectives, the grant required a colleague from another discipline, a colleague from the same discipline/department, and/or an undergraduate or graduate student on each research team. Two specific changes in the grant requirements over time are relevant to this chapter: (a) the required inclusion of student researchers on all grant teams and (b) the requirement that the topic of the SoTL work be about promoting learner autonomy (for a broad definition, see p. 149).

The former change, requiring student members, began long before Illinois State University became involved in the latest 3-year Carnegie Academy for the Scholarship of Teaching and Learning (CASTL) Institutional Leadership Program initiative where we are members of the themed group on student voices in SoTL. Given our university's strategic plan, we believe that students should be involved in SoTL work and that we should become partners with students to study teaching and learning. Parts of the goals in our strategic plan include that we work "with students as partners in their educational development inside and outside of the classroom, so that students come to appreciate learning as an active and lifelong process," and we focus "on each student as an individual, with unique educational needs and potential. The University is dedicated to placing the learner at the center of teaching and scholarship," and we prepare "students to be informed and engaged citizens who will promote and further the collective goals of society. The University promotes active learning experiences through which students will gain an awareness and understanding of civic engagement as a lifelong responsibility" (Illinois State University, 2009a).

One way to involve students in SoTL has been to engage them as active research partners in our internally funded SoTL grant program. In an earlier 3-year CASTL institutional initiative (2003–2006), Illinois State was the lead institution in a cluster of 11 schools working on supporting SoTL at the campus level. Part of this earlier initiative also involved efforts on the various campuses to include student voices in SoTL, including but extending beyond students as research subjects.

We also began the internal SoTL grant program by leaving open the topics or teaching problems addressed in the studies. Later we required that topics link explicitly to any of the values or actions in our institutional strategic plan. Then a few years ago, we made the decision to focus the grants on promoting learner autonomy. The reasons for this change included faculty concern (expressed in teaching workshops and other settings) about low levels of learner autonomy demonstrated by our students, goals in our strategic plan that were connected to the construct of learner autonomy, and some potential international connections related to SoTL work on learner autonomy. For definitions and a bibliography related to learner autonomy, see http://www.sotl.ilstu.edu/castlAahe/autoWeb.shtml. The language about learner autonomy used on the call for proposals read as follows:

> For FY07, projects must focus on the topic (broadly defined) of promoting learner autonomy. Autonomous learners are students who take responsibility for their learning, are willing to collaborate, partnering with faculty and peers in their learning, are reflective about their learning, and are involved in shared governance. Autonomous learners are strong life-long learners.

Thus investigators sought student voices in at least two ways via this grant program: (a) Students are, most often, the research participants in the studies, and (b) all studies involve one or more undergraduate or graduate students as co-researchers. Some grants also engaged student voices by inviting students to serve as pretest or pilot participants, as validity checkers of qualitative data, as attendees who could respond to the studies in local presentation situations, or as members of classes where faculty shared SoTL results and how they would like to apply them in that class.

We believed there would be a connection between student voices and promoting learner autonomy. That is, it was our hope that the research results would prove useful in enhancing the learning autonomy of students across campus and, perhaps, their ability and willingness to voice their ideas on teaching and learning. In addition we believed that the students serving as co-researchers on the grants would become more autonomous learners from the experience of serving as co-researchers and from what they learned about learner autonomy.

Examples of Learner Autonomy Studies From the SoTL Small-Grant Program

The use of a broad definition of learner autonomy has facilitated incorporation of the concept into grant recipients' work in disciplines as diverse as agriculture, anthropology, business, construction management, criminal justice, education, health sciences, and psychology. These fields offered uniquely enriched opportunities for learner autonomy and the expression of student voices. In this section we discuss four SoTL small-grant recipients' research projects emphasizing the objectives of the studies, their methods for exploring learner autonomy, key results, and types/examples of student voices. While SoTL small-grant funding opportunities have resulted in a number of studies worthy of report, we selected these for the diversity of discipline, content, and method, as well as for the variety of ways they express student voices. The works identified and discussed below have been summarized from project profiles available from the Illinois State University SoTL Web site, http://www.sotl.ilstu.edu/castlAahe/autoWeb.shtml.

Agriculture Applied Science Application

The first project involved a six-person research team: two faculty members and four students from the Department of Agriculture. The overarching theme of the project was to examine autonomous learning techniques employed in an applied science curriculum. More specifically, the researchers sought to facilitate learner autonomy by creating an opportunity for students to link discipline-based theory to practice through real-world application. The future of the field of agriculture is largely dependent on educating and maintaining qualified and trained individuals in the industry, many of whom have no prior agriculture or farming experience, so practical application is key.

The project consisted of training a sample of students to be quality evaluators of food animal products (e.g., pork loin) and testing their application of the gained knowledge and skills. Undergraduate students enrolled in two courses, Foods of Animal Origin and Introduction to Meat Science, and voluntarily participated in a study using an experimental design to examine visually the quality of pork loins treated with natural antioxidants. Researchers drew 46 students from both classes and randomly divided them into control and experimental groups.

The control group received in-class information and instruction about meat quality as part of the standard course curriculum. The experimental group received the in-class information and instruction and completed a hands-on laboratory component to provide practical experience. Both groups completed a pre-test involving the subjective analysis of pork loins after a specific number of days of refrigeration. Investigators used Likert scale responses to rate the color, firmness, and marbling of the meat. Upon completion of the course material addressing meat quality, both groups completed a post-test meat quality assessment. The intent of the exercise was to encourage students in the experimental group to self-educate by drawing on the hands-on training opportunities they had participated in and the additional practical experiential knowledge they had gained.

Faculty were using the practical hands-on lab training component of the course as a model for inclusion in the curriculum that would enhance self-directed student learning using real-world application in meat science. Despite statistical results showing no significant effect of treatment between the pre- and post-test, the researchers remain optimistic that hands-on training integrated into the curriculum via the lab component of the course, and based on a strong theoretical rationale, should promote learner autonomy.

The *student voices in this project* came into play via the student researchers' working on the funded SoTL project and by the students engaged as study participants in the research. Student researchers had an opportunity to gain experience working on several tasks (e.g., developing and setting up experimental stimuli, observing outcomes, interpreting data) with faculty serving as mentors. Student participants were able to inform efforts to enhance and improve curriculum through their willingness to serve as research subjects. The feedback from participants has influenced discussions about the future direction of curriculum and instruction in the Department of Agriculture.

Active Learning in Criminal Justice Research Methods

The second SoTL small-grant-funded project discussed here involved a three-person research team, two faculty members, and one student from the Department of Criminal Justice Sciences. The team explored the use of active learning techniques and the research project model (using a student-driven, real-world research project to address a problem salient to the campus community) to facilitate learner autonomy and teaching social science research methods courses in criminal justice.

More specifically, the project assessed how the implementation of tiered assignments and the incorporation of the research project model affected students' attitudes toward the course, their perceived competencies across an array of research-oriented skills, and perceived relevance and importance of research methodology in students' everyday life using pre- and post-test data collection. The in-class project accentuated what Littlewood (1999) refers to as *reactive autonomy*—autonomy that does not create its own direction but once the direction has been initiated can enable learners to organize their resources autonomously to reach the end goal.

A total of 67 students from four sections of criminal justice research methods courses participated in the pre- and post-test assessments, linked through unidentifiable code names. The pre- and post-test questionnaires sought to measure several key concepts: (a) motivation level/attitude toward active learning/learner autonomy, (b) skill level as it applies to seeking new information and becoming a lifelong learner, and (c) perceived skill level and ability to apply information taught as part of the class. The questionnaire concluded with open-ended feedback questions.

In part, the researchers hypothesized that students exposed to this method of learning would have more favorable attitudes toward conducting research and using active learning skills. They further hypothesized that students would increase their autonomous learning skills (seeking new information, developing critical thinking skills, and applying new information), providing a framework for lifelong learning.

The results of the complete statistical analysis revealed several significant and informative findings. Student interest in research methods improved significantly from the pre- to the post-test, and engaging in hands-on activities as their preferred method of learning increased significantly from the pre- to the post-test while studying by themselves significantly decreased. Students also revealed they are significantly more likely to regard published research and cited research skeptically than before they took the course and participated in the research project. Students also felt significantly more confident in their own abilities to conduct a small research project if requested by an employer. They were also significantly more cognizant of the impact research findings have on their life and significantly more confident in the ability to discern scholarly research sources from nonscholarly sources.

Student voices in this project emerged in part because of the student researcher who assisted with developing the tiered assignments, instructing the student participants on how to undertake each assignment, and conducting analysis and interpretation of the pre- and post-test assessment data. The student research participants in the project were able to express themselves on several occasions via the various data-gathering strategies. Their responses had a direct impact on course instruction and in developing curriculum for future course offerings.

Process-Oriented Guided-Inquiry Learning and Clickers in Health Sciences

A three-person team, two faculty members and one student from the Department of Health Sciences, conducted the third small-grant-funded project discussed here. They designed the project to evaluate the use of two specific learning modules from a total of 26 modules in a general education course on environmental science. The two modules were to promote learner autonomy in the course using Process-Oriented Guided-Inquiry Learning (POGIL) with a student classroom response system using handheld remotes known as *clickers*. They expected that POGIL and clickers would increase learner autonomy by creating a student-centered, discovery-based learning experience in the classroom.

The two POGIL learning modules implemented in the course addressed pesticides and biodiesel. Both sessions were hands-on interactive activities for the students taking the class. The pesticide module used hands-on simulations while the biodiesel module used a series of laboratory demonstrations. Classroom clickers allowed students opportunities for input into each demonstration and experiential learning component associated with the modules.

The researchers then sought to examine the impact of the POGIL modules on students' learner autonomy. Students in several sections of the course (sample size ranged from 58 to 161) participated in the assessment, which involved comparing quiz scores following POGIL units of the course and non-POGIL units of the course. The researchers hypothesized that students exposed to POGIL modules would be more likely to engage in the topic and self-study resulting in better quiz performance. Results suggested student performance did increase after POGIL exposure. Students' exam scores on questions addressed by the POGIL exercise were also compared to previous sections of the course prior to the incorporation of POGIL in the course curriculum, and the results were similar though not statistically significant. The researchers also sought student feedback on the POGIL sessions through anonymous clicker responses recorded for two questions addressing the helpfulness of the hands-on pesticide and biodiesel modules. On a Likert scale ranging from strongly agree to strongly disagree, students responded positively to both modules.

While not all the results were significant, the authors note that POGIL appears to show promise in large lecture hall settings for promoting learner autonomy. The student co-researcher who worked on many research tasks expressed *student voices in this project* by assisting in developing the two POGIL modules (brainstorming ideas, pre-testing the modules), assisting in implementation of the two POGIL modules particularly for the biodiesel POGIL module where experiments are involved, and conducting class observation as a qualitative measure of the effectiveness of the modules. This student has also gone on to present and publish work related to aspects of this SoTL-funded research, some of which received an award. In addition, the student participants enrolled in the courses with POGIL modules provided feedback on the experience and helped inform and enhance the learning experience for future students.

Teacher Immediacy, Learner Autonomy, and Student Achievement

The fourth and final SoTL small-grant-funded project involved a three-person research team, two faculty members and one student from the psychology department. The project explored learner autonomy and student achievement motivation as a function of teacher immediacy and student attachment. More specifically, the work sought to identify variables in the student-instructor relationship that predicted the quality of that relationship and subsequent student achievement and learner autonomy. The researchers noted that self-directed students reported stronger supportive relationships with instructors. Therefore, identifying which variables might predict these supportive relationships with instructors is important. The researchers emphasized the connection between teacher immediacy—verbal and nonverbal behaviors and cues exhibited by instructors in the classroom that serve to foster positive student-instructor relationships—and student achievement and autonomy.

Two hundred sixty-three full-time college students ranging from 18 to 22 years old completed a series of questionnaires. The questionnaires assessed generalized attachment functioning or attachment security, verbal and nonverbal teacher immediacy, and student-instructor relationship (high or low levels of connectedness with and anxiety toward the instructor). The measured aspects of autonomy included perceptions of confidence and control, and self-directed learning.

The results included a finding that student gender did not appear to affect the quality of the student-instructor relationship, with males and females equally likely to form positive relationships with strong connectedness and low levels of anxiety. Further, a student's attachment security did not appear to improve or impede his or her relationship quality with the instructor. In addition, the verbal and nonverbal teacher immediacy scales predicted different components of the student-instructor relationship, with high verbal immediacy related to high ratings of student-instructor connectedness and high nonverbal immediacy related to lower perceptions of relationship anxiety between student and instructor. Finally, students' achievement motivation and autonomy were predicted by their instructor's immediacy behavior, though this was only the case when the student also felt a strong relationship connection to the instructor and had low levels of perceived relationship anxiety.

The research in large part supports the theoretical foundations of the study. Autonomous self-directed student learners reported strong and supportive relationships with their instructors. The researchers identified several salient characteristics that serve to develop and strengthen that supportive instructor-student relationship. Verbal and nonverbal immediacy foster feelings and impressions of student-instructor connectedness, which in turn relate to student confidence, control, and self-directed autonomous learning.

Student voices in this research were expressed by the student researcher who assisted with the data collection and interpretation and has gone on to continue working with the instructors. The student participants, those enrolled in the courses where the questionnaires were completed, provided insightful information on the teaching and learning dynamic of the classroom and helped to examine what, up to this point, had been largely a theoretical discussion.

Results From Interviews With Student and Faculty Members of the SoTL Grant Program Research Teams

Using different questions for student and faculty team members, we conducted face-to-face interviews with faculty and student researchers. Our main focus was on the experiences and outcomes of the students working on these projects from the faculty and student points of view. After multiple attempts to contact all those involved, we were able to interview 18 individuals (6 students and 12 faculty), gathering data on 11 of the 13 grants awarded over the 3 years in question, 2005–2006, 2006–2007, and 2007–2008. Our student co-author interviewed the six students, and two of the faculty co-authors split the task of meeting with and interviewing the faculty. For all six student interviews we have feedback from at least one faculty member from those students' teams. Interviewers took detailed notes during the interviews, then reviewed and added to those notes immediately following each interview. Given time constraints, we interviewed grantees from 2007–2008 before they had all their results in place and before they were able to follow through with presentation and publication efforts. Nevertheless, we believe the findings from those interviews are compatible with those from the 2 previous years.

All but one faculty member were appreciative to have had student collaborators; one faculty member acknowledged adding a student initially only because the SoTL grant application mandated that a student be on the team. This faculty member remained uncertain about the benefits of the student co-researcher to the student or the project. Faculty recruited student collaborators in ways that are not surprising. They tapped undergraduate students and graduate assistants they knew and trusted and thought might have an interest in the project. Faculty tended to favor students who had completed the classes that were to be the focus of the learner autonomy research.

Beyond their student collaborators, faculty also needed students as research participants. Subject pools ranged from general education classes to doctoral students. Though in most cases students could opt to participate in or abstain from the activity or data gathering, in some cases students had to participate for learning and informal assessment. In all cases, however, investigators were to obtain institutional review board approval to use any data in a SoTL project that would go public.

Overall, the students and faculty were positive about the outcomes of their research partnerships focusing on learner autonomy. All the interviewed students relished the chance to be a vital part of a real research endeavor. Student collaborators learned by performing a number of important research steps. Although the project ideas were initially the province of the faculty, most faculty members invited these students very early in the process to help think of ways to measure learner autonomy via a classroom project and to assist with writing the proposal leading up to proposal submission. Some student collaborators were the sole student assistant on the project, while others were part of a student team working with faculty. Student tasks performed during the projects varied widely. Examples of tasks performed included researching best practices for whatever the project involved, acquiring items needed in class (such as used cooking oil), setting up in-class experiments, collecting data in class from student research subjects by means of questionnaires or observation, coding the results, thinking about what it all meant regarding advancement of learner autonomy of classroom students, and co-presenting and co-publishing the results for wider audiences. One student collaborator used the grant project as the basis of her master's thesis and another for her undergraduate thesis.

Student voices came through loudly and clearly as faculty turned to their student colleagues for advice and innovative ways of doing the research. Faculty were effusive in their praise of collaborating students when we asked for actual examples of contributions the students made, useful ideas that faculty either did not think of, or things faculty could not have done on their own. And, as one student stated, "collaboration was the best part of the experience" because it included "pulling on each other's strengths." Some of the projects involved questionnaires, and students helped immensely with questionnaire preparation. In one project the student co-researcher suggested asking whether students thought it mattered if a professor spoke with an accent or whether he or she made them feel more comfortable in class by offering extra credit assignments. Another project's student voice came to the fore-front after the participants piloted the questions. The student, thinking as a student, told the professor the group had to change the wording of some questions because students would misinterpret what they were seeking. When it came time for administering those questions to the students, the student colleague did all the interviews. Looking back, the student's profes-sor admitted that she could never have gotten her students to open up in the way their peer was able to. A third grant involved a semester-long, classwide research project with sequenced subassignments. The student collaborator had taken the class before and was able to provide "unique insights about how the assignments would be received by students in the class and how challenging they were." Finally, the student who collaborated on a classroom demonstration project proved to be invaluable, as she developed a checklist of items needed to conduct the demonstration, created a molecular model from ordinary items around her home (like foam insulation and pool toys) that instructors could show and then rearrange in front of the class, and envi-sioned and performed an observation of students while demonstrations were proceeding.

We also tried to ascertain what benefits the collaborating students received from their participation (see also chapter 6 for benefits and chal-lenges to student voices in SoTL research). To learn about such takeaways, we queried the students themselves and the faculty who worked with them on the projects. In general, the responses were similar; but students had more to say on the subject than the faculty. Both groups pointed out the value to the student of doing the research in the company of people who have research experience. Students felt uniformly that they became better researchers in the process. Some credited their project with either propelling them to the next stage in their life (e.g., graduate school) or planting the idea that graduate school or a teaching career ought to be something for them to consider. A nontraditional (over the age of 25) female student said she used to be the sort of undergraduate who sat in class, took notes, and tried to be invisible. Following her participation as the sole student collaborator on her learner autonomy project, she now strives to involve herself in class and as a result feels "more confident." Students and faculty applauded the fact that several of these students were able to present results of the research at profes-sional meetings, including some at distant venues.

Given that learner autonomy played a key role in the projects during these 3 SoTL grant years, our student co-author probed deeper with her student interviews, asking, "[Has] this learner autonomy project altered your views on the ways you approach learning?" Of all the questions on the student survey, this one elicited the most commentary. Interviewees spoke of now needing less faculty direction on research projects, of gaining a major measure of academic independence after the success of the learner autonomy project, of being better prepared for graduate school than other members of their cohort, of managing time more efficiently, and of seeing how mistakes made can lead to better ways of doing research the next time. One young woman, now in graduate school, was able to serve as "an author on multiple convention papers along with the grant project" and took the opportunity "to go to UNLV [University of Nevada, Las Vegas] to present the project to other schools." She still cherishes the "professional relationships" she was able to forge with these faculty mentors at Illinois State. In the words of another student researcher, he "became an autonomous learner by doing so much [on the project]" by himself. He was able to "learn from past mistakes" and now "definitely" functions more autonomously as a graduate student.

Are the learner autonomy projects altering the classroom landscape at Illinois State? We asked the faculty members what they are changing and whether their departmental colleagues are adopting new practices based on grantee experiences. In the case of grantee classrooms and related instructional practices, the answer is a resounding *yes*. They now know better when to add and when to subtract from course content or approaches. For example, a project that brought dynamic demonstrations to the classroom will likely lead to more of this sort of teaching practice for this pair of instructors. Another team sees implications in their classes and perhaps a change in the way their department assesses learning outcomes for its matriculated majors. For the most part, on the other hand, grantees felt their department colleagues have not shown much interest in the project outcomes. Sometimes that lack of interest derives from the fact that only the grantee faculty members teach a particular course. One pair mentioned they experience much more interest in their SoTL work on learner autonomy at national conferences than in their own department. They see colleagues at distant conferences "writing down things they say" about their learner autonomy projects and "people ask questions" of them afterward.

Going public was a requirement of accepting these grants throughout the 3 years. Presentation at the annual Illinois State Teaching-Learning Symposium was mandatory, as was submission of an article to a print or online outlet. The 2007–2008 call for proposals included a requirement for uploading a "web snapshot" of the project onto the Illinois State SoTL Web site. We wondered how the teams' faculty members were dealing with these mandated outcomes of their grant. All grantee faculty members we spoke with seemed energized by going public. Faculty members, often with students as co-presenters or co-authors, are taking multiple opportunities to spread the word orally and in writing. Some of the earliest recipients have published grant-related papers, and numerous articles are under review or in revision or preparation. One National Science Foundation grant application is a direct outgrowth of a learner autonomy project from the 2007–2008 round of Illinois State's SoTL grants.

Student voices clearly contributed to the quality of these projects. In addition, students and their faculty teammates expressed gratitude for the chance to push the instructional envelope a little further in search of ways to get students to want to learn on their own either as part of a class or entirely separate from the classroom. As one professor put it, these projects are a great way to mentor students as researchers and can truly be "career changing" for faculty members and students.

Conclusion

These SoTL small grants had two major purposes. First, the funds were to help research teams learn about promoting learner autonomy and self-directed learning in a particular discipline or class or set of students. Second, the grants were one way to obtain student voices in SoTL by involving students—as research participants and as research partners or collaborators—in SoTL projects.

We learned several things about promoting learner autonomy through these projects (links to additional information on these learner autonomy projects via brief reports and Web snapshots can be found at http://www.sot l.ilstu.edu/castlAahe/autoWeb.shtml). For example, more than one of the projects found some support for the role of hands-on application, connections between theory and practice, and active learning in promoting aspects of learner autonomy. Involvement in original research and/or inquiry-based or discovery-based learning was also beneficial. There was limited evidence that providing some structure and support or scaffolding for students engaged in these types of assignments was an important characteristic of the tasks. Finally, instructor behaviors (teacher immediacy) can have an impact on students' feelings of connectedness and reduced anxiety and then result in students' greater autonomy in terms of confidence, sense of control, and self-regulation.

We close by offering some tips or best practices for involving students in formal SoTL research (see also McKinney, 2007 and advice in other chapters in this volume). In our experience, it is best to require (by making funding contingent on doing so) student members on the research teams and a description of the student roles as part of the grant proposal. In this way teams guarantee at least one student collaborator and invite him or her into what will more likely be a meaningful role if considered beforehand. In addition, faculty and staff researchers should identify student collaborators early and involve them from the start of the project, even in helping to write the grant proposal. Faculty can find students in a variety of ways, but approaching students who seem interested and qualified and have already taken the class the project focuses on, or are in the class where the data collection will take place, seems to work well. It is best to involve students who will be at the university for more than another semester or two; in this way, they can see the project through and share their voices in the interpretation and making-public phases of the work.

Student voices, of course, will not emerge sufficiently if we only assign the students trivial and/or clerical tasks; rather, these partners must have the opportunity to engage in meaningful and challenging aspects of the project. Students will often need training and guidance for their roles in the project, but we should also treat them as collaborators and as individuals with useful insights to offer. We must create a climate that allows and encourages the students to offer their valuable voices and to raise questions or express concerns about the project or their roles. Students should attend any research meetings or research/writing circles. Faculty and staff researchers should compensate their student partners with funding, travel, academic credit, co-authorship, letters of reference, and future opportunities. Certainly, the chance to co-present and co-write outcomes of the project is important for student learning and provides yet another opportunity for student voices to resonate in SoTL work.

We believe this grant program of SoTL research studies involving students as members of the research teams is one way to hear and respond to the voices of students in SoTL. In addition, the grant program is a way to encourage greater learner autonomy in student SoTL researchers as well as in the future students in the classes studied and beyond.

Note

1. We thank the authors of our other institutional chapter in this book, Patricia Jarvis, Gary Creasey, and Derek Herrmann, as well as our "critical friends," Megan Otis, Joyce Hammond, and Jessie Moore for their comments on an earlier draft of this chapter.

References

Illinois State University. (2009a). *Educating Illinois: Core values.* Retrieved July 20, 2008, from http://www.educatingillinois.ilstu.edu/plan_sections/core_values .shtml

Illinois State University. (2009b). *The scholarship of teaching and learning.* Retrieved July 15, 2008, from http://www.sotl.ilstu.edu

Littlewood, W. (1999). Defining and developing autonomy in East Asian contexts. *Applied Linguistics, 20*(1), 71–94.

McKinney, K. (2007). *Enhancing learning through the scholarship of teaching and learning: The challenges and joys of juggling.* San Francisco: Jossey-Bass/Anker.

McKinney, K. (2008). Broadening SoTL involvement and application via SoTL grants: Moving toward greater impact. *The International Commons, 3*(2), 7.

II

CAPTURING STUDENTS' LEARNING

Tom Drummond and Kalyn Shea Owens

This is a story of how documentation enables all of us to listen more deeply to the student experience, hear students' voices again (and again), and reconsider teaching and learning. We wish to illustrate how documentation provides the opportunity for faculty to revisit their teaching, and for students to revisit the choices they make in the moments they struggle to learn so that everyone involved in education more fully understands how faculty and students grow toward more competent and more intentional ways of being.

We videotaped a selected learning encounter where a small group of 1st-year chemistry students worked together to attempt to understand a challenging concept. We watched the recording and converted one section, a part we thought most puzzling, into still images and transcribed dialogue using Microsoft Office PowerPoint 2003. The result was a "capture" of one slice of their struggle to understand the chemical concept of charge distribution. Slowing it down in photos and text allowed us to listen more closely, to see learning unfold, and to reflect upon their learning and our teaching. The capture allowed us to talk about what we could see of the student experience and co-construct the meaning we saw in it. This documentation (see Figure 11.1), and the subsequent discussions among students and faculty, has transformed our pedagogy and transformed our conceptions of what we do as leaders and participants in education.

We share here a portion of that capture. We offer it as an example of a step all faculty can take to develop more effective pedagogical practices. This work shifts the paradigm, as Barr and Tagg (1995) described, from a discourse based in teaching, the *instructional paradigm*, to an alternative discourse based in learning, the *learning paradigm*. We believe that faculty who gather this kind of documentation take a step toward a new ideal of what school can be for each and every participant—faculty and students.

A paradigm shift challenges people to let go of old ways. According to Barr and Tagg (1995), we have a choice to retain our inherited role as instructors placed at the center and justified to assume the responsibility for content, sequences, texts, and the evaluation of students. Or we have a choice to think of our role as creating settings with opportunities for encounters at just the right level of disequilibrium, at just the right time, in just the right conditions, and over time transport these encounters to greater levels of sophistication. We operate in this latter role when we become willing to take the time to listen to the student experience in learning.

Our story is an example of this listening. We are attempting to put the learner at the center of our investigation and shift the focus from being faculty who are concerned about covering content to being faculty in a reciprocal relationship with our students in reflective practice. As we work toward disarming the power differential between our students and ourselves, we cherish the opportunity we have to help each other learn. Just as the learners are learning, we faculty are learning how to provide opportunities and how to facilitate. As we make the transition from old ways of thinking toward a pedagogy based in reciprocal relationships, a truly deep listening, and a view of the student as powerful and capable, we find that we lack the words to describe this more democratic, open interdependence among faculty and students. We offer our story as a provocation to develop a new kind of discourse, one that differs significantly from the ways we customarily describe what we do in higher education.

Our work arose from a faculty seminar group led by Carnegie scholar Jim Harnish who introduced us to the Student Voices cluster in the scholarship of teaching and learning (Carnegie Academy for the Scholarship of Teaching and Learning [CASTL] initiative). He invited a group of faculty and students to meet regularly to talk about learning. As members of that group, we became intrigued about helping each other investigate the student experience. We had these questions in mind: How can we create the conditions that enable everyone, all of us, to gain each day in school? How can we enable each other to be and understand in new ways?

One of us (Owens) teaches chemistry; the other (Drummond) teaches early childhood education, which is currently deeply influenced by the municipal preschools in Reggio Emilia, Italy. The Italians' remarkable example has challenged the world to transform all schools into amiable, democratic places of culture. Howard Gardner, then a co-director of Project Zero (see http://www.pz.harvard.edu/History/History.htm), a research group at the Harvard Graduate School of Education, became interested and eventually became friends with Loris Malaguzzi, the founder of the Reggio Emilia schools. In subsequent years, Reggio and Harvard faculty exchanged ideas about how the documentation of children's thinking and work can provide an opportunity for teachers to reflect upon and to listen more deeply to the children and each other. Project Zero and Reggio children published this way of listening in a collaborative book, *Making Learning Visible* (Renaldi, Giudici, & Kreschevsky, 2001), in which they explored what it meant to document learners and the learning group. In joining our disciplines of early childhood and chemistry, we brought the Reggio model of inquiry to higher education. We invite you to examine our example and reflect upon the possibilities it suggests.

We conducted our study in the context of a year-long general chemistry sequence for science majors at North Seattle Community College, an urban commuter college with an enrollment of about 6,000. We designed the curriculum to actively engage participants in co-construction of chemical concepts, using drawing as a means to represent and debate theories, and offering challenges to apply newly constructed knowledge to more complex problem solving and explanations of real-world phenomena.

A Capture: Representing the Charge Distribution of Sulfur Dioxide

The students in this capture (Figure 11.1) were encountering the chemical concept of molecular polarity, the forces at work that explain why oil and water do not mix, a foundational understanding for 1st-year college chemistry. The students had already been introduced to two other ways of representing molecular polarity: partial charges and the dipole moment arrow. Immediately prior to the sequence we recorded, the instructor had presented an additional way to represent the polarity of a molecule that uses a color scheme to symbolize positive and negative charge distribution.

FIGURE 11.1

Representing the Charge Distribution of Sulfur Dioxide

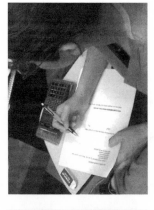

Matthew: Couldn't sulfur dioxide be double-bonded with each oxygen? But it would still have a lone pair, wouldn't it?
Melissa: Yes. It would have two lone pairs.

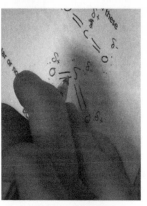

Matthew counts the electrons in his Lewis structure representation:
Two, four, six, eight, twelve.

Melissa's Lewis structure drawings of CO_2 and SO_2
Sulfur is full, though, with double bonds. Isn't it?

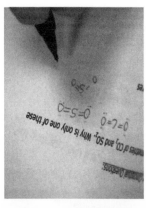

Melissa counts hers also: Two, four, six, eight. Eight for sulfur.
Matthew adds: Plus the lone pairs, because sulfur comes below.

Shana: I thought there was a resonance structure. (Pause.) I don't know. Is it?

Shana redraws SO_2 below her initial attempt. She now shows it bent and with one double bond and one single bond representing its resonance structure.

(continued)

FIGURE 11.1
Representing the Charge Distribution of Sulfur Dioxide (continued)

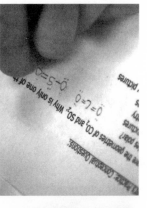

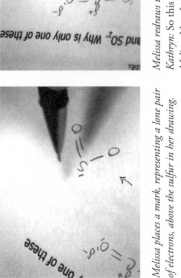

Matthew says aloud as he sketches: Double bond. Double bond. Oxygen. Oxygen.

Shana erases one of the bonds and two dots she had placed above the double-bonded oxygen in her initial drawing.

Melissa: Oh. I see.

Shana: You need one double bond and one single bond.

Matthew (gets it now): Making a resonance structure.

Kathryn (now sees it also): Raising her eyebrows.

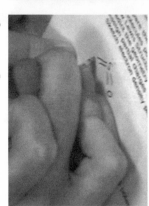

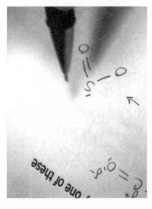

Kathryn: Yes. You could have the other oxygen. Yes.

Melissa places a mark, representing a lone pair of electrons, above the sulfur in her drawing.

Melissa redraws the molecule.

Kathryn: So this is a little more complicated. This is coming over this way . . .

Melissa: Now I am confused. This is coming over this way . . .

Shana: Has more electrons.

Shana listens as Melissa talks:
So the single oxygen bonded molecule . . .
The single-bond oxygen is the more . . .

Melissa: Isn't O$_2$ . . .
I really like working in groups, because I
don't have to think of these things all on
my own. It works so much better for me.

Kathryn: Has more electron density.

Kathryn: No. More negative.

Melissa: It's more positive.

(continued)

FIGURE 11.1

Representing the Charge Distribution of Sulfur Dioxide (continued)

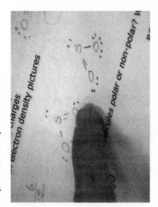

Kathryn ponders her drawing, which is correct with all bonding and nonbonding electron pairs.

Matthew: There are more electrons over there that aren't being shared.

Kathryn: It seems like this part of it is more negative and this is more positive.

Kathryn: She says on here, "Predict the geometry."

Melissa: Well, we did that with this dot structure.

Kathryn: But that's not exactly telling us . . . Because the lone pairs affect the geometry too, right?

*Kathryn: So, assigning partial charges . . .
This would be . . . .*

She pauses and looks away to consider this.

*Kathryn: It's just bent. That's what the
geometry is, right? So Melissa, it's just bent,
you don't need to . . .
Well, you want to. (Laughter.)
Melissa: Yeah, I want to. This is more fun.*

*Shana adds the negative partial charge
symbol δ to her drawing.*

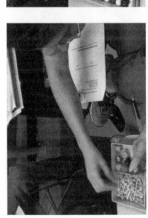

*Melissa begins building a model of the SO_2
molecule in order to visualize the structure.*

*Shana: Three charge cloud, right?
The electron cloud.
Matthew: Right.*

(continued)

FIGURE 11.1

Representing the Charge Distribution of Sulfur Dioxide (continued)

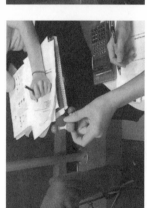

Melissa holds up the model, 2 green oxygen bonded to the red sulfur. What do you call this?
Matthew and Kathryn reply in unison: Bent.

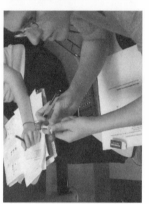

Melissa: Oh.
It's got the lone pairs and a double bond.

Matthew: It's just like water.

Kathryn: This is the sulfur. We have to designate. This one is going to be the one with the double bond, okay?

Kathryn: You're right, Matthew. It's like water. It's just bent.

Melissa points to the double-bond side: So this is the more negative stuff.

Kathryn: I don't think so, because . . . Is that right?
Matthew: Yeah, yeah, you're good.

Kathryn: The one with the double bond only has two lone pairs out here and this one has three lone pairs out here.

Kathryn: So, it's more . . . the double-bond side is more . . .

Kathryn refers to the sulfur with her ring finger: And this one has a lone pair out here too.
Melissa: I got completely confused.

Shana: More positive.
Kathryn: Yes.

Matthew: I'd say the sulfur is more . . . Well, only one lone pair compared to the two. But then the double bond . . .

(continued)

FIGURE 11.1
Representing the Charge Distribution of Sulfur Dioxide (continued)

Shana: They look the same.

Kathryn: If you were going to do the cloud, if you were going to do the color diagram . . .

Kathryn points to the single bond: this part of the molecule would be more red . . .

Shana: Maybe I should draw it.

Kathryn points to the double bond: and this would be more blue. Do you think that is right?

Shana: What if it was like this? She colors a portion blue . . .

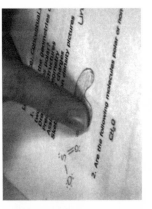

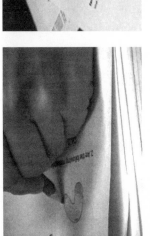

Shana describes her drawing: I have the double bond and this part kind of red . . .

and three other areas red.

Shana: And then this part very negative. And it is bigger. It is lopsided.

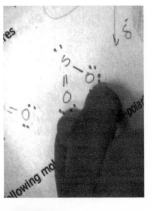

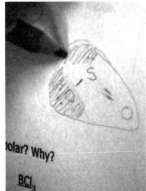

Kathryn: You know, you guys, as far as drawing this, maybe we . . . I mean, if you look at how many electrons are around the oxygen at this side . . .

Kathryn colors her drawing.
Melissa: Yeah. That's what I did. On the outside. And the red more toward the center. Like that.

Kathryn: It seems like out here it would be kind of blue.

(continued)

FIGURE 11.1
Representing the Charge Distribution of Sulfur Dioxide (continued)

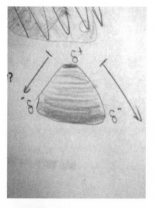

Kathryn: Maybe it's just a shape like this that is blue up here and red down here.

Kathryn: It is simpler than what we thought. More red is toward the oxygen.

Kathryn: So this one I'm going to cross off.
Kathryn completes the new drawing with dipoles and partial charges represented.

Shana considers her drawings.

Shana: I hope this is not on a test.
(Laughter.)

Melissa completes her drawing showing the resultant single dipole arrow.
Now all members of the group have correctly represented the molecular polarity three ways: dipoles, partial charges, and electron density

An understanding of the chemistry concepts is not essential to an understanding of what is happening in the capture, Figure 11.1, for everyone brings a unique way of seeing. Chemists may see it one way; the students themselves, faculty in other disciplines, and administrators may see it differently. The words and pictures enable observers to view and re-view what these students do as they encounter something they do not fully understand. In this sequence, the students wrestle with how to represent with colors the charge distribution in a molecule of sulfur dioxide. We observe Matthew, Melissa, Shana, and Kathryn as they draw diagrams of the molecule sulfur dioxide. Carbon is symbolized with a C, and sulfur is symbolized with an S. Molecular bonds are represented by lines, and the nonbonding electrons are symbolized with dots. We invite you to read this sequence slowly. Even without understanding the chemistry, one can gain insight into how understanding is co-constructed and how representation enables learning to be visible.

Our Reactions to What We Saw

When I (Owens) first reviewed this capture, four understandings came into view for me the chemistry instructor. I was pleased that in the end all members of the group seemed to achieve a satisfactory drawing, even if a full understanding of polarity awaits later study.

1. *It isn't about the answer.* The group seemed to adopt ideas on the basis of an unspoken satisfaction; all they needed was to be right at least for the moment. Being right according to an external standard was almost irrelevant. Oddly, only Shana had her textbook open. There was little interest in looking up the right answer or asking me. Rather than seek an authoritative source, they seemed to prefer building on what each person presently understood. It was as if they *had* to start with what they thought they knew. That sharing brought a unifying energy that sustained their interest in clarifying and building on existing threads of conceptions. They seemed to enjoy the power of moving forward using their own mind in their own way.

2. *The different languages of representation offer different views.* When the students focused on the Lewis structure representation (the drawings in the first 24 frames of the capture), they continued a line of thinking that only considered how the lone pairs of electrons and the double versus single bonds might help them predict molecular polarity. I did not realize that the Lewis structure would be as distracting as it was. It was difficult for them to move

away from this way of thinking because of this way of illustrating their thinking. The shift forward in their work occurred when they used other languages of representation. Kathryn said, "She says on here we have to predict the geometry." Saying it was "bent" allowed them to concentrate less on the electrons and more on the whole molecule. Later, Shana said, "Maybe I should draw it." Once the group represented the molecule as one shape using colors to represent charge distribution, it seemed relatively simple for them to get a drawing that was colored correctly using the framework of electronegativity as well as molecular shape. It is fascinating to me how each form of representation provided a new perspective in thinking, and how at the same time each presented limitations to thinking.

3. *It is shocking how little faculty know about what actually happens for students during the act of learning.* What was most striking to me was how much I normally miss of how the students are thinking. I routinely move from group to group and base my understandings of what is happening on brief snippets of conversations and quick glances at the representations the students have created. I often make the assumption that if the students have a reasonable drawing on their paper, they are beginning to understand. This opportunity to see their entire wandering path was fascinating and informing. In the full 140-frame sequence, I was able to see the connections they made with each other and the way they used their uncertain understandings to build new ones. Their focus on the lone pairs of electrons on the oxygen atom, which led them astray, is now in my thinking. It has already helped me better present this material.

4. *Connected knowing is essential.* I saw the importance of the care they gave to each other. It appeared that these students, although they had never worked together before, were able to stay personally connected. Everyone's contributions were valued. Everyone took risks to present ideas and conjectures. Often they phrased their contributions as questions or made tentative statements in the form of a question. Although each student spoke in brief phrases, almost in shorthand, it was enough to sustain the inquiry and challenge the creation of meaning in the others. The capture enabled me to see how small things moved the group's focus one way then another, cohesively, like a flock of starlings. The social dimension of group participation, interpersonal responsiveness, and openness to others was essential for achieving a deeper understanding of the content. It would be impossible to do this alone.

The Group's First Response to Being Videotaped

Even though we followed the protocol required by our human subjects review committee, we remained concerned about the impact of videotaping on these students. As they were getting their coats and gear packed we kept the camera on and asked them about their experience of being watched on camera. The following is a transcription of what they said:

> *Melissa:* I think working interactively is the greatest way to learn. I really like the teaching style here, because I always feel so encouraged. Even if I make a mistake, I feel "don't give up!"
>
> *Kathryn:* If I am doing this on my own, I just try to get the right answer. When I am doing it in a group I feel like I have to explain why I am thinking something a certain way. Sometimes I am wrong, but explaining it to others allows me to understand it more.
>
> *Melissa:* It seems more conceptual and a lot less abstract. To talk about it and look at these things, put them together and pull them apart, enables me to create an idea that I can back up with scientific information. It is more tangible, and I remember it. It is a lot more fun, too.
>
> *Shana:* I have had teachers where I had to memorize, memorize, and memorize, and then it was gone. I still remember all we did last quarter with Kalyn because it was so interactive. Not that I think chemistry every day of my life, but I actually think about chemistry ideas in the car.
>
> *Matthew:* Kalyn should teach math. I could really use this in math [laughter].
>
> *Melissa:* It really matters to me that she is taking the time to find out how we really learn. Really, who does that? [She turns to talk directly to the lens of the camera.] Thanks, Kalyn!
>
> **Shana:** Yes!

We were relieved to see that the students thought the opportunity to struggle together to understand polarity was valuable and accommodated their differing styles of learning. The result for them was a more durable understanding. The camera apparently was of little concern. Rather than being an interference, videotaping was seen as proof the instructor cared about how they learned.

The Class's Response to Viewing the Capture

Once we converted the raw video footage to slides and had signed releases in hand, we showed the resulting capture to the entire class. The participants, Matthew, Melissa, Shana, and Kathryn, read aloud their own statements on each slide. Afterward we asked the class members to write their responses to seeing the capture. Here are representative samples.

Students in the Capture

- "Watching the PowerPoint gave me an opportunity to be an observer of my own learning process. I was able to see how I took risks by saying that I was confused or making an assumption that later appeared to be inaccurate. I like the ability to brainstorm with others. I feel this experience has "kicked it up a notch" in regard to my learning process. I feel this experience has helped me exceptionally grasp the concepts in this chapter."
- "In watching the PowerPoint of our interactions, I was surprised by how much we built our understanding together. How much we completed each other's sentences. I could see how each person in the group contributed the pieces that they understood or misunderstood. (Even the misunderstandings were very helpful to our learning.) Having to explain how we thought really helped us clarify our thoughts."

Students Not in the Capture

- "The slides pointed out how learning something is a step-by-step process. You make a connection and then based on that you can make another connection and you figure things out by building on these connections."
- "Watching them figure it out, though, confused me a bit. They brought up questions that weren't clearly worked out that left me more confused. I feel that I now need to review the material! Which maybe is actually a good thing!"

Anecdotally, I (Owens) saw a qualitative change in the way the students worked together throughout the rest of the year. The students who were in the capture became highly regarded, for others often asked them for their contributions. I also think this experience was a metacognitive transformation for everyone in the course. After seeing the capture, all the students seemed to see themselves as people who figured things out together. Instead of coming into the chemistry classroom with a sense of uncertainty, they became scientists eager to contribute to the next challenge. Learning chemistry became a game they enjoyed playing together. It is as if the opportunity to *see* themselves as members of a learning community enabled them to find their own voice and view themselves as powerful and competent.

Final Video Interview of the Students Who Were in the Capture

At the end of the year, just after the students took their final exam for general chemistry, we invited them to be interviewed on videotape. Unfortunately, Melissa was absent. Since we did not know exactly what we were trying to discover, we simply offered an opportunity for them to talk about whatever they liked. Mostly they discussed the course and how it was taught, but this segment of the recording pointed to their metacognitive transformation.

Matthew: This experiment was on learning something new and expanding it. I saw benefits across the board. I was looking forward to coming to class afterward, not that I wouldn't anyway, but it was more so. There was more of a group dynamic, the whole class was more group oriented, and I felt that my ideas were being discussed in a small circle, as opposed to sitting, hearing and going home.

Shana: As I read through the printout of the slides I thought, "Well, this is my learning process, obviously. You can't really be embarrassed about how you learn." You are going to make mistakes. It is normal. I think everybody in the class understood that. There is no need to be worried about that.

Kathryn: I thought it was interesting to see myself and see how I interact with other people. It is another piece of learning.

Matthew: Showing it to the rest of the class was fun. I am glad it wasn't in motion pictures, because, well, it's like answering machines: something about hearing your own voice bothers me. But I didn't have a problem seeing the pictures. That was fine. That's how I have been projecting myself for 20 years, and it has been fine, so why change now? [laughter]

Shana: People still like me.

Matthew: Exactly. Obviously I am interacting with people so something is not completely wrong [laughter].

Matthew: I just read through my lines. As I said them aloud I was thinking, "Yeah. That would be something I would say." Looking back at it again, rehashing in your mind what you said, and saying it again even, shows you the path. Once you have done it once, see it again, and go back and do it again, you can see where it diverges. When you think about it, you see, "I could have gone this way, but I chose to go this way." You can see the chain of events that I followed.

Kathryn: Being videotaped and seeing ourselves was helpful because it showed me how I interact with other people. I agree that for the most part I think, "Well, that's just the way I am." But I reflected on myself. Maybe I could change some things. I could be a better listener or not jump in so quickly and things like that. It is part of life to be able to do that kind of group work.

We note how the capture, and reflection on the capture over time, advanced their understanding of their own learning. They saw themselves as people willing to take risks, willing to be uncomfortable with not knowing, and valuing their interactions with others as essential to their own success. They demonstrated they were, in feminist terms, *constructed knowers*, the highest level in the epistemology of voice described in *Women's Ways of Knowing* (Belenky, Clincy, Goldberger, & Tarule, 1997) as well as in the epistemology offered by Perry (1981) as "commitments within relativism" (p. 79). We concluded that our listening to the voices of these students supported the development of not only their cognitive and ethical growth but also their voice. They were no longer passive receivers of knowledge transmitted by authoritative teachers; they were co-inquirers.

Conversations Among Faculty

We wondered what our colleagues would see in this capture, so we offered the other chemistry faculty the opportunity to discuss it. We recorded those discussions too. The discussions ranged over a variety of topics, but these words of one of our colleagues in the chemistry department pointed out how faculty can learn from other faculty's documentation.

- "It was interesting to watch and reflect on my own style. I see myself jumping in more often to get them on the 'correct' thing, but way too soon. The more I watched the more I appreciated the process these students went through. I realized that they didn't need the instructor's help really. I see my personal tendency to want to go in there and get them in the right direction, but that would have been detrimental to their learning process. I would have taken them off: my mind would have taken over the problem solving which is not conducive to their learning. I can see a flaw in my own style. Watching that, seeing how well they did, and knowing how I would have reacted if I had been around them going, 'No. No, you guys. Wait.' was a good experience."

- "Sometimes when I give students a project like that where they work in groups to solve it, I feel I am approached by them with 'tell me the answer.' That is what they have wanted, so I have done that for them—a lot. What I see in this capture is very contrary to what happens in my class, because they were just diving in. They were not seeking out the instructor, even when she was close by. I thought that was pretty great."

We have seen the effects of this documentation on ourselves, the students we listened to, their peers in the classroom, and our own colleagues in teaching. Capturing the voices of students in their learning opened an opportunity for everyone in the learning enterprise to reflect upon how they think about what they are doing and what they value in their classrooms and schools. By closely examining the events of the classroom in a concrete and tangible way, we open the possibility to discover what we might otherwise miss, and with others, create enhanced practices that benefit everyone's learning.

In the documentation we saw how Matthew, Melissa, Shana, and Kathryn were being powerful and capable. We saw how their learning did not proceed in a linear way but in fluid and tentative wandering. We saw how the construction of knowledge was a group process where each was nurtured by the conjectures and responsiveness of others—some confirming, others questioning—toward new connections and understandings. We saw how each person had unique contributions, paces, and strategies.

In our discussions of the documentation with other faculty, chemists and nonchemists, we enjoyed hearing the distinctive perspectives they contributed not only about the students but also about their own understanding of teaching. These conversations about pedagogy were comparable to the students' conversations about polarity. We can only imagine what would happen if we had general agreement that the conclusions concerning the students in the paragraph above also applied to faculty learning how to teach. If we thought faculty were powerful and capable, if we thought learning to teach was a fluid and tentative wandering, if we understood pedagogy as a group process nurtured by the conjectures and responsiveness of others, we could design opportunities for faculty to create meaning together in groups, talking together to co-construct an evolving understanding of pedagogy engagingly enabled by documentation.

Listening to the Voices of the Students

Documentation enabled us to access the voices of the students and construct together the meaning of what it is we heard. We recognize that we cannot really know what is happening in the mind of each unique and diverse student. We may do our bits of listening and watching, but we only see what we are open to in that moment, and our perceptions and expectations filter what we see. If we can admit that our selectivity is a fact, we must also admit that we are necessarily uncertain about how best to teach. We must be willing, therefore, to embrace that uncertainty and position ourselves less as "masters of the truth" and more as creators of space where those directly doing the learning can act and speak on their own behalf.

We offer our method of documentation as a tool to allow faculty to see and listen more carefully and to participate in making meaning and reflection. These are essential processes in learning and growth. This form of documentation recognizes and values complexity and context while remaining concrete. Most remarkably, the reflective dialogue it stimulates directly alters the educational experience; students change and faculty change without a need to convince anyone of anything. John Dewey (1938) describes the work this way:

> A primary responsibility of educators is that they not only be aware of the general principle of the shaping of actual experience by environing conditions, but that they also recognize in the concrete what surroundings are conducive to having experiences that lead to growth. Above all, they should know how to utilize the surroundings, physical and social, that exist so as to extract from them all that they have to contribute to building up experiences that are worthwhile. (p. 40)

Documentation not only leads us to what is worthwhile, it has a direct, profound effect on the participants themselves. It presents incontrovertible evidence that students are indeed powerful and capable—especially when they are confused or mistaken—which enables all of us involved in education to work together to modify the conditions of the educational experience so their capabilities can flourish. With documentation students can revisit their own experiences; they can see how aspects of their participation illuminate complex and multiple actions, social and conjectural, and sustain the knowledge-building process. In documentation faculty and students can see learning, not as something the students do but as something faculty and students do together. Documentation creates an opportunity for reciprocity that moves us a step forward toward an ethic of practice.

Just like these students, we faculty need our communities for co-construction with each other of what is beautiful and satisfying in higher education classrooms. We are aware of beautiful teaching and learning when we see it or live it, without the need for numbers or measures. We all face the need for something to examine together, something specific, complex, and nuanced to reflect upon to honor the differences in the way each of us perceives the world and expresses ideas. We all face the problems of working cooperatively together, of solving problems, of examining habitual practices, bringing self-critical awareness of our own uncertainties, and of offering, in mutual comfort, tentative conjectures and hypotheses. We all face co-creating a future through our interactions in the present. We all face an expectation that we wish to move toward an ideal, a beautiful dream of our own abilities to do well.

How do we nurture that space? We suggest documentation—gathering traces of experience in photographs, recordings, and products—to enable faculty and students to revisit events in our classroom, contribute our differing views of what we see, make meaning, create shared values, and transform our expectations and culture. The dialogues we have about the meaning we see in the documentation gives higher education a learning focus: to create an amiable space for learners and faculty, not only for the transmission of what the faculty know but also for knowledge building by students and faculty alike. The more diverse perspectives we have engaged in making meaning about the complexities captured in documentation, the more we can help each other learn about what it is we do. We all gain when we listen to student voices.

References

Barr, R. B., & Tagg, J. (1995). From teaching to learning: A new paradigm for undergraduate teacher education. *Change, 27*(6), 13–25.

Belenky, M. F., Clincy, B. McV., Goldberger, N. R., & Tarule, J. M. (1997). *Women's ways of knowing: The development of self, voice, and mind* (10th ed.). New York: Basic Books.

Dewey, J. (1938). *Democracy and education.* New York: Simon & Schuster.

Perry, W. G. (1981). Cognitive and ethical growth: The making of meaning. In A. W. Chickering & Assoc. (Eds.), *The modern American college* (pp. 76–116). San Francisco: Jossey-Bass.

Renaldi, C., Giudici, C., & Kreschevsky, M. (Eds.) (2001). *Making learning visible: Children as individual and group learners.* Reggio Emilia, Italy: Reggio Children.

NOT THE CONCLUSION

Moving From *Engaging* to *Sustaining* Student Voices

Carmen Werder and Megan M. Otis

C. Werder (CW): Who's going to start writing this conclusion?

M. Otis (MO): Well remember, this is *not* the conclusion. We agreed that we don't see this volume as the definitive word on student voices. This work (we hope) will keep going long after this book is published. And since the people contributing to it certainly are not the only ones engaging student voices, the chances look good for that happening. So this volume, including this conclusion, is simply our contribution to what we see as an ongoing dialogue about creating partnerships with students in the study of teaching and learning.

CW: Yes, all agreed. This is *not* the conclusion for all those reasons. Now who's going to start writing? I mean we've worked hard to create some sense of parity as co-editors, so who's going to take the lead right now?

MO: I think you should start because you're a faculty type and writing expert.

CW: No, I think you should start because you're a student type, and you can more easily tap into the expertise that learners bring.

MO: No, I really think you should start. You have been doing this work a lot longer than I have. That's why I *let* you put your name as first co-editor (*joking*).

CW: (*smiling*) Fine, I'll start. I would like to propose that we move from thinking about this work as *engaging* student voices to *sustaining* student voices in ever deeper and broader ways. While engaging is a good word to describe the intensity of the work, it doesn't convey a sense of its ongoing nature.

MO: I really like that idea. After all, we can engage students once, but it doesn't necessarily mean that we continue to engage them over time. *Sustaining* means *supporting* in such a committed way that something will not only live but thrive. This volume illustrates some ways we have initiated partnerships with students at our institutions and opens the door to finding new ways to strengthen and extend that commitment. Another reason I like *sustaining* is that it also means *to uphold as valid*. Over the years I've worked with you, we've talked to many people about student voices, and while many are really receptive and accepting of the concept, some people seem to think it's not really valid, that it isn't *real* scholarship. So I think this book is really cool in that it demonstrates how scholars in so many fields and from so many different kinds of institutions across the country are upholding student voices as a valid and important version of the scholarship of teaching and learning (SoTL).

CW: Oh I'm glad you're bringing up what we agree is a faulty assumption: Inviting students in as co-inquirers somehow diminishes the scholarship. That's part of why I was so eager (in chapter 2) to highlight the idea of this scholarship's taking many forms, including embodied ones, where the dialogue—the ongoing conversation itself—embodies the scholarship and deserves attention. When I think of the work of our contributors, such as the studies our colleagues Kathleen McKinney and Patricia Jarvis (and their colleagues) have been doing for so long on the concept of learner autonomy in the contexts of sociology and psychology, I also note how deeply embedded in the disciplinary scholarship and how sophisticated this co-inquiry with students can be.

MO: You're so right about that, and our contributors often demonstrate how we can find theories to support and validate student voices across a number of different disciplines. I think it's really clear throughout the book, and especially in the first part, "Foundations." For example, the co-authors of chapter 1 point out a number of relevant theories prominent in philosophy, much as you and your co-authors bring theories from communication, and my co-author and I bring a theory from anthropology to bear in our discussions. We also have contributors from a range of other disciplines: education, education psychology, English, geography, history, human services, mathematics, psychology, sociology, special education, theater arts, philosophy, and political science. And faculty in all those disciplines have found numerous ways to validate student voices in theory, method, and methodology.

CW: Yes, the impressive range of disciplines represented in this book points to how *readily transportable* the notion of students as co-inquirers in studies of teaching and learning can be. This disciplinary range also suggests that students could be actively studying their own learning at all levels of education—not just postsecondary. Call it metacognition, call it SoTL, or simply call it learning writ large—I've come to think we can engage students as co-inquirers in any context.

MO: Makes sense. So if the ultimate goal of SoTL at the college level is to improve disciplinary learning, then doesn't it make sense that students ought to be active partners in investigating their own learning whenever possible, not just in special cases? If students are passive participants in research on teaching and learning, just the research subjects or objects of research, how can we expect them to be anything but passive learners in their chosen field of study? I think this book gives evidence that students can take active roles in the study of teaching and learning across disciplinary boundaries.

CW: Before we leave this conversation about the usefulness of talking about this work in terms of *sustaining*, there's another big piece: Not only are we offering ways to validate students as co-inquirers, we're also quite clear it's the presence of student voices that sustains us. I know all our contributors agree: Students inform and inspire our scholarship. They sustain us.

MO: Yes, I agree. In moving from the language of engaging to sustaining, we imply we want this work not only to continue but to flourish. Even if it looks as if this work were already widespread judging from our contributors' work, what's been done so far is really just the ground floor of what might be a castle (with a nod to our Carnegie Academy for the Scholarship of Teaching and Learning [CASTL] mentors). The co-inquiry needs to be more pervasive. It needs to be more typical. Right now, what we're doing still seems unusual, so it needs to become the norm.

CW: Why are you so sure it isn't the norm?

MO: Well, one thing that shows it's still atypical is when I go to SoTL conferences I'm only one of a handful of students.

CW: But how do you know that small number is truly representative of what's really going on within the institutions themselves when it comes to involving students as co-inquirers? I mean it's not easy for faculty to get funded for these conferences, and it's even more challenging for students.

MO: I don't know for sure, but students at these conferences still seem kind of like monkeys in a zoo: "Oh, look at those students, look at all the things they can do." Often, it seems like a superficial display. At times, students aren't really regarded as equal intellectual partners.

CW: Is that the way you feel you've been perceived in the process of writing and editing this book?

MO: No, not always. But at times I felt some of the contributors considered me somewhat of a "junior" editor, and they mistakenly thought that ultimately the final decisions would fall exclusively to you. I remember how often people would send e-mails to you, and they wouldn't include me. But you always made sure to send me a copy, and you asked others to make sure they sent their e-mails to both of us.

CW: Did that sense of being less than equal seem to happen earlier in the process then? Did you notice some kind of change after a while?

MO: Yeah, after a while people just sent their e-mails to me and left you out (*snickering*).

CW: Very funny.

MO: Actually, I think it was easier for other people to eventually accept me as a full co-editor than it was for me. It was really hard to accept my own authority and expertise. I couldn't escape the near-constant fear that someone was going to object to my editing role and say to me, "What do you know about SoTL or editing or anything? You're only a grad student, and you don't even have your master's degree yet. I felt like I kept seeking your reassurance (and the reassurance of the other contributors) that my ideas and suggestions were useful, and I was constantly surprised when people took me seriously as a coeditor.

CW: So at what point did you accept that you were being taken seriously?

MO: I don't think I've fully accepted it. But that's OK, right?

CW: Would it help if I took my name off the book cover?

MO: Absolutely. Megan Otis, Sole Editor Extraordinaire. Sounds good to me.

CW: OK, now that you're so full of yourself (at least for the time being), I must tell you that I haven't always felt secure in my role as co-editor either. I had never edited a book before and often sought reassurance that I was doing it right. But for me, somewhere along the way, I began to recognize where my expertise would fit best as a co-editor. I felt affirmed in my expertise on writing issues since I've spent a lot of years teaching writing. So it made sense that I would often take the lead on suggesting stylistic revisions. And I loved that we were comfortable enough with each other that I could do that and even assert my expertise at times.

MO: Yeah, because I'm still not sure what passive voice is.

CW: Are you serious??

MO: No, I'm kidding! But that was really funny to me (since it was such a big deal as we were editing together). I mean I never really knew much about grammar and syntax and stuff like that before, so I learned a lot working alongside you. Besides, I think there were lots of good things that I brought as a co-editor too.

CW: Like what?

MO: Well, for one thing, I brought a student perspective to the whole book. I was very, shall we say, *sensitive* to the language used to talk about students in this work. For example, I've been a very vocal advocate for using the plural *student voices* rather than the more commonly used singular *student voice*. Students are amazingly diverse in their perspectives, and they don't all speak with one single voice. So it's been really important to me to consistently use the plural form of the term throughout this volume to recognize that diversity of views. In editing I also tried to help retain a real sense of the student co-authors' voices in the writing. It was important to me that our readers could actually *hear* students in the chapters. That's why at times I resisted "fixing" the grammar or changing the word choice if it meant losing a sense of real students talking. And I also brought years of experience in SoTL itself. For a student, it's remarkable that I have been able to do this work for quite a long time—3 years as an undergraduate and almost 3 years as a graduate student.

CW: Yes, but 6 years is a long time for anyone to be involved in this work given that even though it's been going on under different rubrics, it wasn't until the last decade or so that CASTL has promoted it in *student voices* terms. Of those past 10 years, you've been involved for 6 of them, so you're a special case. You have an ongoing student perspective and a long history with this scholarship.

MO: Well, you've had an even longer history with the CASTL Student Voices initiative because you've been involved since the beginning.

CW: Guess that's why we've made a good team. At the same time, of all the expertise that you bring individually, I believe it's your fundamental *student-ness* that is most crucial to the work. While I know that I will likely not ever have the good fortune to work with a student over time and in such significant ways as I have with you, I truly think it's the alliance with students—regardless of the level of their experience or sophistication with SoTL—that we must sustain. Often when I've gone to conferences with students, others will observe how special these particular student participants are, how "self-selected" they must be. But the truth is that many, perhaps most, of the students who have been most actively engaged with this work at our institution were not particularly engaged learners at the outset. Because so many have had a chance to participate through various avenues (not only through traditional leadership paths such as student government), they have often been pretty typical students, and some have even felt disenfranchised and indifferent to their learning before becoming involved. So I'm convinced that all students, in varying roles of course, can work with faculty in this scholarship, can gain from it, and can contribute to it. We faculty types quite simply need current students to *remind* us of the consequences of how we approach teaching and even how we talk about students, as well as of the openings we give (or don't give) for students to speak their learning minds.

MO: I agree that student voices in this work are very important, but I don't want to suggest that faculty voices are any less important. Faculty bring a greater understanding of how to be scholars than students because they've learned how in their academic training. They also bring their rich disciplinary expertise and their experiences as teachers and as learners. Because of their position in their institutions and the fact that research by faculty is more respected, they also bring more legitimacy as scholars. Typically, when students do research, it's more of an exercise in skill building than creating new knowledge. It's like "pretend scholarship," but when students work with faculty as partners, it is real scholarship. And that's an incredibly transformative learning experience for students. I know it has been for me.

CW: I think it can be equally transformative for faculty too. Because once you've done co-inquiry with students on teaching and learning, it seems somehow inadequate to do it without them. I know that's been the case for me.

MO: Why?

CW: Because when you're studying teaching and learning with students, you get different kinds of questions (often more significant ones), different language, and different kinds of analyses. And because the study is grounded in real students' lived experiences, the results seem better, more genuine. Most importantly, when students are research partners, I see a whole different impulse when it comes to translating the findings into practice. Students won't let our scholarship just sit there. They insist on it not being only knowledge for the sake of knowledge; we need to translate that knowledge into making learning better.

MO: I'm glad you used the word *translate*, because that's another thing I really value about student-faculty co-inquiry. They can translate for each other. Faculty are fluent in academese, which students are learning. Students are Academese as a Second Language (ASL) speakers. And, like anyone learning a new language, they need chances to chat and try out the language that faculty speak with ease. Similarly, students speak a student dialect, or studentese. Students can more easily speak to and understand other students. So when developing SoTL research methods, for example, if faculty want the most solid results they would do well to frame their questions in language that students can readily understand. So it's a reciprocal translation process.

CW: Yes, I have often heard faculty who've worked with students in SoTL say that their instruments, like questionnaires and interview questions, become much more refined because of student co-researchers' insights. A student can read a survey question with the eyes of a student respondent and see when a particular item will be hard to understand and can suggest how to rephrase it. I also think, as you've suggested, that student researchers gain from this translation process because they learn how to talk the talk and walk the walk of scholars. So this collaboration can provide benefits to all. In fact, one little study at our institution suggested that students who have served as co-inquirers on teaching and learning gain a greater sense of connection with the institution and a heightened sense of ownership for their own education.

MO: While faculty-student partnerships in this study certainly do have a lot of benefits for all, we don't want to give the impression that it's all roses and sunshine, do we? This work is often challenging, as our contributors have frequently acknowledged.

CW: Yes, very challenging, even downright frustrating. I mean, even you and I, who have worked together for such a long time, have had our challenges in co-editing this book. Most pointedly, I remember when you were offering editing suggestions for the chapter I co-authored, and you brought up your strong reservation about the Kenneth Burke epigram.

MO: Oh man, I was so scared to say anything to you about that epigram. I knew how much you liked it, but I was concerned about your use of it in the chapter because I had always heard the phrase "put in your oar" used in a negative way—meaning "to interfere or meddle"—and I thought that it went against the whole point of your chapter. Part of me didn't want to say anything; I was afraid to challenge your expertise. So I did a little more research to see if there was any validity to my concern, and I found several dictionary entries that confirmed the meaning of the idiom as I saw it.

CW: And when you showed me your findings, partly because I was scurrying between meetings and partly because I thought the chapter was close to being done, the only thing I heard was, "I don't like your epigram." My initial thought was, "Oh great, there goes the epigram and so goes the chapter." That sense of panic triggered some anger too. I was also startled that of the many times I had encountered that Burke quotation in the literature, no one had ever suggested that it had any negative connotations. In fact, I had seen the parlor image Burke uses in multiple rhetorical contexts as a positive metaphor for scholarship itself. So I was trying to reconcile the new information you were giving me with what I had experienced before, trying to reconcile your expertise/experience with mine.

MO: At the time, I felt you were telling me I was wrong and completely dismissing my concern. I was quite hurt.

CW: Really, I wasn't simply dismissing what you were saying. I was just trying to understand because it was totally new information to me. If I hadn't used this same quotation before, and if I hadn't seen it used before with a positive connotation, I would have responded differently.

In some ways, you might even interpret my response as a respectful one because it wasn't simply a knee-jerk deference to you as a student but rather a considered questioning. I was also hurt that you took my response as a criticism of your experience, that I was flat out saying you were wrong, that I didn't hear or value what you said. As I look back, I think our ability to negotiate our way through these troubled waters epitomizes the work itself. What's telling about the whole anecdote for me is how absolutely essential this kind of reflective dialogue is to our collaborative scholarship. We can't just talk about the work, we also have to talk about *how* we do the work. We have to talk about who we are and how we negotiate our expertise together.

MO: Yes, and I think it's really important that this communication part of working together be explored even more in the future.

CW: Yes, we definitely agree that the way we enter into dialogue with each other requires much more investigation—indeed, it's part of sustaining this work. In fact, I still can't get over the definition of sustainability that I encountered this past year when one of our science faculty quoted an environmental scholar defining it as "an ongoing dialogue about what matters to us" (Robinson, 2008). I love that. I love the idea of sustaining this work in terms of its being a process, not a destination, and that it centers on what we most care about.

MO: And that's another reason why this is *not* the conclusion. What matters to us can change over time.

CW: I guess one of our main invitations to others, then, is to keep this dialogue going, not only by continuing to work with students in studying teaching and learning but also to investigate more deeply this co-inquiry as a process. What does this co-inquiry look like when it works well? And how do we know? Somewhere along the line, a colleague remarked on his collaborative work with students saying, "I'm learning how to listen *differently* to students." Intuitively, I immediately agreed that it does involve a different kind of listening. On reflection, I think this different kind of attention means listening with respect for the experience and expertise that learners bring. Studying how this listening to student inquirers might be different from simply attending to learners' needs could be a wonderfully fertile ground for more research. What do you think—are you up for it?

MO: Count me in, though you know I can't stay a student forever. Maybe one day I'll be a faculty member like you, doing this work from that angle. For now, here's hoping more and more student voices are heard in SoTL as we sustain the work—and each other.

Reference

Robinson, J. B. (2008, September). Keynote address at the 16th International Conference of the Society for Human Ecology, Western Washington University, Bellingham.

CONTRIBUTORS

Lindsey Altvater is a 2009 graduate of Elon University. She studied English with a concentration in secondary education and worked in the university's Writing Center. In return for the scholarship support of the North Carolina Teaching Fellows program, Lindsey is currently teaching English at a public high school and hopes to pursue a master's in library and information studies eventually.

Jeffrey L. Bernstein is professor of political science at Eastern Michigan University. His research interests include public opinion and political learning, citizenship education, and the scholarship of teaching and learning. His publications have appeared in the *Journal of Political Science Education, Politics and Gender,* and numerous edited volumes. He was a 2005–06 Carnegie scholar with the Carnegie Foundation for the Advancement of Teaching and currently serves as secretary for the International Society for the Scholarship of Teaching and Learning.

Stephen Bloch-Schulman is an assistant professor of philosophy at Elon University who works at the intersection of political philosophy, collective responsibility, and the scholarship of teaching and learning. He is cofacilitator of the Hannah Arendt Circle and is chair of the Speakers and Awards Committee of the American Association of Philosophy Teachers.

Gary Creasey is a professor of psychology at Illinois State University. He has published peer-reviewed book chapters and journal articles in developmental psychology and in the scholarship of teaching and learning journals and is the author of one book. He serves on three editorial boards and conducts research on attachment, learner autonomy, and student-instructor relationships. He gives presentations on a regular basis at teaching and learning conferences and recently received an Outstanding College Teaching Award at his institution.

Deborah G. Currier serves as chair of the Department of Theatre Arts at Western Washington University and teaches the Drama in Education series, Theatre History, Dramatic Literature, and Theatre for Social Change. She directs the university's Summer Youth Theatre Institute and the Multicultural Outreach Tour. Her current research is in developing a theatre for social change major, with cross-curricular studies in theatre, human services, and sociology. Currier holds a PhD in theatre arts from the University of Oregon.

Alexa Darby, PhD, is an assistant professor in the Department of Psychology at Elon University specializing in educational psychology. Her research focuses on teacher candidates' perspective toward high-poverty schools and ways to reduce stereotyping. She also conducts research on teacher emotions during educational reform. Darby weaves her main goal of mentoring undergraduate research throughout her research agenda.

Betsy Newell Decyk, PhD, serves as the university ombuds for the California State University, Long Beach, community. She has taught philosophy and psychology and has served as project leader for the Faculty Center for Professional Development. She is executive director of the American Association of Philosophy Teachers and in-coming chair of the Teaching Committee of the American Philosophical Association. She has made presentations at many teaching and learning conferences including Carnegie colloquia and International Society for the Scholarship of Teaching and Learning conferences. She has participated in the Carnegie Academy for the Scholarship of Teaching and Learning Student Voices projects since 2004.

Ayesha Delpish, PhD, is an assistant professor in the Department of Mathematics at Elon University specializing in educational measurement and testing. Her current research focuses on using case studies and other inquiry-based methods to observe ways students advance their quantitative reasoning and critical thinking skills.

Tom Drummond is an instructor in early childhood education at North Seattle Community College where he has taught since 1974. Based on years of using videotape to examine teaching and learning in the campus laboratory school, he created unique courses for teacher education based in co-construction of understanding, representing to learn, and the reciprocal relationship between documentation and metacognition.

Denise Faigao is a graduate student in social work at the University of Chicago, School of Social Service Administration. She received her bachelor's in psychology at Illinois State University where she was first introduced to the scholarship of teaching and learning by two professors she worked on a grant with and who helped her become involved with this book.

Peter Felten directs the Center for the Advancement of Teaching and Learning and is an associate professor at Elon University. His latest publications explore questions about historical thinking, student learning, visual culture, and faculty development. He serves on the Membership and Communication Committee of the International Society for the Scholarship of Teaching and Learning and on the editorial board of the *International Journal for the Scholarship of Teaching and Learning.*

Kelly Flannery is an undergraduate working toward her bachelor's degree in philosophy at Elon University. She was introduced to the scholarship of teaching and learning through various independent study projects over the past two years with Stephen Bloch-Schulman, a philosophy professor at Elon. She plans to attend graduate school in philosophy.

Ellen E. Gutman is a PhD candidate in the Department of Political Science at the University of North Carolina at Chapel Hill. Her research interests include public opinion and political behavior, voter knowledge and information, and elections.

Joyce D. Hammond, PhD, is a longtime participant in Western Washington University's Teaching-Learning Academy. Her scholarship of teaching and learning work with other faculty and students ranges from faculty research in their service learning courses to faculty/student joint investigations and presentations of textbook images, participatory action research methodology, and digital storytelling. As an anthropology professor, Joyce teaches qualitative methods, visual anthropology, gender studies, and tourism. She has previously co-authored two other articles with the university's graduate and undergraduate students.

Derek Herrmann is a graduate student in the psychology program (developmental sequence) at Illinois State University. He became involved in the scholarship of teaching and learning while working on a grant with two of his professors/mentors, and he has come to contribute to this book through another professor/mentor. After earning a master's degree at Illinois State, he plans to enter a PhD program in developmental psychology and become a university professor.

Ashley Holmes is a doctoral student in the rhetoric, composition, and teaching of English program in the Department of English at the University of Arizona. Before entering the doctoral program, she taught as a lecturer in the English department at Elon University where she completed the service-learning course redesign project described in chapter 7. In addition to the scholarship of teaching and learning, her research interests include composition theory and pedagogy, service learning, teacher education, visual rhetoric, and teaching with technology. Holmes is particularly interested in ways to collaborate with students on curriculum design and development.

Mary Taylor Huber is a senior scholar at the Carnegie Foundation for the Advancement of Teaching. A cultural anthropologist, she has written widely about cultures of teaching in higher education. She was co-editor with Sherwyn P. Morreale of *Disciplinary Styles in the Scholarship of Teaching: Exploring Common Ground* (Washington, DC: American Association of Higher Education, 2002), *Balancing Acts: The Scholarship of Teaching and Learning in Academic Careers* (Washington, DC: American Association of Higher Education, Carnegie Foundation, 2004), and co-authored with Pat Hutchings *The Advancement of Learning: Building the Teaching Commons* (San Francisco: Jossey-Bass, 2005).

Pat Hutchings is vice president of the Carnegie Foundation for the Advancement of Teaching. She has written widely on assessment, peer collaboration and review of teaching, and the scholarship of teaching and learning. Her publications include *Ethics of Inquiry: Issues in the Scholarship of*

Teaching and Learning (Menlo Park, CA: Carnegie Foundation for the Advancement of Teaching, 2002), *Opening Lines: Approaches to the Scholarship of Teaching and Learning* (Menlo Park, CA: Carnegie Foundation for the Advancement of Teaching, 2000), and with Mary Taylor Huber, *The Advancement of Learning: Building the Teaching Commons* (San Francisco: Jossey-Bass, 2005).

Patricia Jarvis is a professor of psychology at Illinois State University. She has published peer-reviewed book chapters and journal articles in developmental psychology and in scholarship of teaching and learning (SoTL) journals. She serves on two editorial boards and conducts research on learner autonomy. She is involved in the SoTL movement through the Carnegie Academy for the Scholarship of Teaching and Learning program, is a SoTL summer scholar at Illinois State University, and is a member of the International Society for the Scholarship of Teaching and Learning.

William Harrison Lay has been a classroom educator and curriculum development specialist for nearly 40 years. Beginning his professional career as a high school language arts teacher, he has spent the past 25 years as an instructor at Western Washington University's Woodring College of Education. He currently designs and teaches courses in educational foundations, coordinates new teacher recruitment and retention efforts, and develops sustainable mentorship programs for the college.

Deborah T. Long is professor of education at Elon University where she serves as director of the Elon Academy, a college-access program, and coordinator of civic engagement. She has a history of publications and presentations at professional meetings on the topics of teacher cognition, curriculum development, problem-based learning, content integration, and the scholarship of teaching and learning. Her areas of expertise include curriculum development and instructional design.

Catherine King is associate professor of psychology and associate director of the Center for the Advancement of Teaching and learning at Elon University. In her teaching, educational development, and research efforts, she seeks to understand and facilitate students' intellectual and psychosocial development in the context of their college experiences.

Mary Knight-McKenna, PhD, is a teacher educator at Elon University specializing in literacy and special education courses. Her research focuses on teacher candidates' responses to academic service learning experiences in high-poverty schools. She also researches teacher candidates' reflections on interactions with family members of diverse students. Knight-McKenna involves undergraduate research students in this work. As she uses research outcomes to inform her instructional practices, she invites students to engage in the scholarship of teaching and learning process.

Christopher Manor is currently a sophomore philosophy major attending Elon University. He believes his lack of formal experience in the field of teaching and learning is an asset for encouraging student/faculty cooperation and hopes to interest other students in the subject. His other scholarly interests include Zen Buddhism, positive psychology, neuroscience, and philosophy, and he hopes to find a career that accommodates all four.

Chelsea J. Martin is an undergraduate working toward her bachelor's degree in political science and public relations at Eastern Michigan University. She plans to attend graduate school in political science.

Jillian Mattera is a 2009 graduate of Elon University with a degree in English and secondary education certification. During her undergraduate years, Jillian was a consultant at the Elon University Writing Center. She also worked with the Elon Academy assisting local high school students with composition and rhetoric. Jillian spent summers as a technical instructor for iD Technical Camps at the Massachusetts Institute of Technology campus. She looks forward to continuing her career in writing and rhetorical studies.

Kathleen McKinney is professor of sociology and Cross chair in the Scholarship of Teaching and Learning Program at Illinois State University. She's involved in the Carnegie Academy for the Scholarship of Teaching and Learning Institutional Leadership Program and was a founding member of the International Society for the Scholarship of Teaching and Learning. She was an editor of *Teaching Sociology*, was a Carnegie scholar, and has received several teaching awards at institutional and national levels. Her latest book is *Enhancing Learning Through the Scholarship of Teaching and Learning* (Bolton, MA: Anker, 2007).

Richard Mihans, PhD, is a teacher educator at Elon University specializing in literacy and social studies education courses. His research focuses on teacher retention. He is particularly interested in beginning teachers and their satisfaction once in the teaching profession. Mihans regularly supervises undergraduate students in joint research initiatives. He also enjoys discovering new ways to include student voices in his teaching and research.

Jessie L. Moore teaches Professional Writing and Rhetoric and Teaching English to Speakers of Other Languages at Elon University. She also coordinates the university's 1st-year writing courses. Her current research focuses on preparing future teachers to support K–12 English as a second language students, scaffolding students' development as citizen rhetors, and supporting faculty writers.

Michael Murphy is an undergraduate student in human services at Western Washington University. He has worked with the Teaching-Learning Academy, Carnegie for the Scholarship of Teaching and Learning Student Voices Institutional Leadership group, and has presented at several scholarship of teaching and learning conferences over the past 4 years. He is currently conducting a case study with another faculty member on classroom disruptions as part of his SoTL research. Michael plans on pursuing a master's degree in either student affairs administration or counseling upon graduation in 2010.

Megan M. Otis is a graduate student in anthropology at Western Washington University. She has been an active participant in the university's scholarship of teaching and learning (SoTL) initiative, the Teaching-Learning Academy (TLA) for 6 years (as an undergraduate and graduate student), and she is writing her master's thesis on the TLA. Megan has been deeply involved in the Carnegie Academy for the Scholarship of Teaching and Learning Student Voices Institutional Leadership group, presented at several SoTL conferences, and is also an active student member of the International Society for the Scholarship of Teaching and Learning.

Emily Regan is part of the 2010 class at Elon University where she will receive a degree in English with secondary education certification. She has started working as a consultant at the campus's Writing Center. Emily is also a member of the English Honor Society, Sigma Tau Delta, and the Elon volleyball team.

Erin M. Sergison is a PhD candidate in the Department of Political Science at Michigan State University. Her research interests include the intersection of religion and political behavior, faith-based and secular nonprofits, local government studies, and public policy issues of morality and science. She was a 2007 Carnegie graduate fellow for the Residential College in the Arts and Humanities at Michigan State.

Kalyn Shea Owens, PhD, is an instructor of chemistry at North Seattle Community College where she has been involved in innovative course design and research on student leaning. Her research focuses on the design of interdisciplinary, community-based curricula for science majors that weaves chemistry, biology, and sustainability into a year-long program. Owens also has a deep interest in documenting students as they socially construct and represent their scientific thinking in a classroom setting.

Erik Skogsberg became involved in the scholarship of teaching and learning (SoTL) and the Teaching-Learning Academy (TLA) in 2003 through a course called "Learning Reconsidered" at Western Washington University. Carmen Werder (the course instructor) later asked Erik to co-teach the course and facilitate a section of the TLA. For the next 3 years, he represented the university at conferences throughout the country, advocating the importance of student involvement in SoTL. Erik graduated from Western in 2006 and went on to receive a master's of arts in teaching degree from Brown University in 2008. He currently teaches high school English in Yelm, Washington.

Michael D. Sublett, a Phi Beta Kappa with a PhD in geography from the University of Chicago, has been a member of the faculty at Illinois State University since 1970. He is the author of various monographs, atlases, professional papers, and reports, many of which deal with aspects of the Midwest. His BA and MA are from the University of Missouri-Columbia. His contribution to this chapter is his first publication dealing with student voices.

Cora Thomas graduated from Western Washington University in 2007 with a communication degree. She has been an active member of the Teaching-Learning Academy (TLA) since 2006 and continues to participate as an alumna. She has presented her scholarship of teaching and learning research at the 2006 Carnegie Academy for the Scholarship of Teaching and Learning Student Voices convening at the University of Nevada, Las Vegas, and also at the 2008 Festival of Scholarship conference on collaborative inquiry at Western Washington. Cora is pursuing a graduate degree in student affairs administration because of her deep inspiration from the TLA.

Jane Verner has been affiliated with Western Washington University's Human Services Program in the Woodring College of Education since 1991. In addition to her classes, she directs the Human Services Program on the main campus, serves as faculty adviser for Students for Social Change, and actively participates in Western Students Against Cancer, Woodring's Diversity Committee, the Teaching-Learning Academy, and Western's Carnegie Academy for the Scholarship of Teaching and Learning Student Voices Institutional Leadership Team.

Jeffrey A. Walsh, PhD, an assistant professor in the Department of Criminal Justice Sciences at Illinois State University, routinely conducts research with his students. He engages in research related to student learning, specifically in academic dishonesty and teacher immediacy, autonomous learning, and the utility of project-based learning in research methods courses. His latest work has been published in *The Journal of Faculty Development* and he has a forthcoming article in the *Journal of Active Learning in Higher Education*.

Luke Ware is a communication alumnus of Western Washington University where he was an ongoing member of the Teaching-Learning Academy, Carnegie Academy for the Scholarship of Teaching and Learning Institutional Leadership Team, and co-coordinator for the 2008 Festival of Scholarship conference on collaborative inquiry. Through independent research and co-inquiry, he modeled ways to embrace student voices. He is a colleague and former student of Carmen Werder, and the pair have shared their findings in various settings in the United States and Canada. He firmly believes pretzels should be a staple in every conversation on teaching and learning.

Carmen Werder directs the Teaching-Learning Academy at Western Washington University where she also teaches rhetoric and directs the Writing Instruction Support faculty inquiry program. As a 2005–06 Carnegie scholar, she initiated an ongoing study of the use of personal metaphors in developing a sense of agency and has interwoven that research with the study of teaching and learning. She has headed the Carnegie Academy for the Scholarship of Teaching and Learning initiatives involving students as co-inquirers in both iterations: the Sustaining Student Voices cluster (2003–06) and the current Student Voices Institutional Leadership Program themed group (2006–09). She has made presentations alongside students at many conferences in the United States and Canada and has been an active member in the International Society for the Scholarship of Teaching and Learning since its inception.

INDEX

Also available from Stylus

Exploring Signature Pedagogies
Approaches to Teaching Disciplinary Habits of Mind
Edited by Regan A. R. Gurung, Nancy L. Chick, and Aeron Haynie
Foreword by Anthony A. Ciccone

"A remarkable achievement that is sure to find its way onto everyone's short shelf of essential books on teaching and learning. The real contribution of the volume lies in the authors' recommendations for how disciplinary fields might develop signature pedagogies that enact and perform the disciplines' core concerns. It also fully demonstrates the claim that teaching, when properly conceived, is exciting intellectual work. Thus, this is the perfect book to give to faculty members who are dubious of 'faddish' education research."—**Lendol Calder**, *associate professor of history at Augustana College, currently represents the Organization of American Historians on the board of the National Council on History Education.*

Disciplinary Styles in the Scholarship of Teaching and Learning
Exploring Common Ground
Edited by Mary Taylor Huber and Sherwyn P. Morreale

Ten sets of disciplinary scholars respond to an orienting essay that raises questions about the history of discourse about teaching and learning in the disciplines, the ways in which disciplinary "styles" influence inquiry into teaching and learning, and the nature and roles of interdisciplinary exchange. Disciplines represented: chemistry, communication studies, engineering, English studies, history, interdisciplinary studies, management sciences, mathematics, psychology, and sociology.

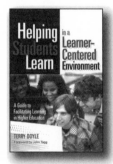

Helping Students Learn in a Learner-Centered Environment
A Guide to Facilitating Learning in Higher Education
Terry Doyle
Foreword by John Tagg

"Terry Doyle's book brings together findings that will enable us to answer what so many college and university faculty members want to know: How do we enable our students to learn to learn (and love it)? If your goal is to develop lifelong learners, this book is a guidebook for your practice."
—**Laurie Richlin**

"This book is brilliant in that it does three things very simply and without unnecessary complexity: it explains why learner-centered environments should be used, how to create them (complete with how to sell students on an approach that will actually help them), and how to tell when students are learning. What is different about this book is that Terry Doyle outlines WHY students will resist this change. His point-by-point guidance on creating a learner-centered classroom incorporates a strategy for bringing the students along as willing participants."—**Todd Zakrajsek**, *Director of the Faculty Center for Innovative Teaching at Central Michigan University*

22883 Quicksilver Drive
Sterling, VA 20166-2102

Subscribe to our e-mail alerts: www.Styluspub.com